The Indian Investment in Family Planning

George B. Simmons
Department of Economics and
Center for Population Planning
University of Michigan

An Occasional Paper of
The Population Council

The Population Council
245 Park Avenue
New York, New York 10017

Distributed for The Population Council by
Key Book Service, Inc., 425 Asylum Street,
Bridgeport, Connecticut 06610.

Standard Book Number: 0-87834-004-1
Library of Congress Catalog Card Number: 75-155738

Printed in the United States of America by The Van Dyck Printing Company,
North Haven, Connecticut.

Contents

List Of Tables

List Of Figures

Preface

THIS STUDY has two basic and closely related purposes. The first is to illustrate an approach to the evaluation of family planning programs. The basic contention is that the use of economic measures provides both a better means of asssessing the overall impact of family planning activities and a better guide to making decisions within the program than the more common demographic or administrative measures of performance. Our second purpose is to apply this approach to the Family Planning Program instituted by the Government of India. During the twenty years since India gained independence, economic policy makers have sought to intervene deliberately in the national economy so as to allocate resources to their best use. One of our basic themes is that allocating scarce physical and human resources to an effort to reduce the number of births taking place leads to economic benefits that far outweigh the costs of the resources used in the process.

The organization of the present study will be foreign to many readers. Our basic purpose has been to undertake an economic assessment of the Program, and the internal organization reflects this concern. As a result those readers who want to know something about particular aspects of the Program will be obliged to search in a number of places. For example, statistics relating to the total number of sterilizations done in India as a whole can be found in Chapter IV, but a break-down by state is given only in Chapter VII.

The book examines the Family Planning Program as an economic investment. Chapter I presents the framework for and the justification of this approach. Chapter II attempts to assess the value of preventing a single birth. Measured in terms of the nation's per capita income, we estimate that the value of a birth prevented is on the order of 7,800 1967–68 rupees. Chapter III estimates the number of births that are prevented by each sterilization and each insertion of an intra-uterine contraceptive device (IUD). Chapter IV combines the results of Chapters II and III with the statistics relating to the adoption of sterilization or the IUD in India to give some idea of the economic return to past investments in family planning. We conclude that the return to expenditures on family planning has indeed been very large; the net gain for 1969–70 may have been as high as Rs. 16 billion, a figure on the same order of magnitude as the total annual amount of foreign aid coming to India during the past few years. Moreover, the ratio of benefits to costs is extraordinarily high—40:1 for 1969–70.

It is not sufficient, however, to show that the number of births occurring in any year will be lower as the result of a certain number of sterilizations performed and IUD's inserted. It must also be shown that, in the absence of the government Program, the same events or equivalent events would not have taken place. It is argued in Chapter V that there was no sign of a demographic transition beginning in India before the introduction of the government Program, and nothing has happened during the past ten years that would lead one to expect, on the basis of the experience in other societies, that such a transition was imminent. The people who have availed themselves of the family planning services offered by the government of India are not overwhelmingly from those classes that initiated the demographic transition in the West. Two kinds of evidence are presented. First, evidence relating to the individual adoptors of the IUD or sterilization is given which shows that they are mostly of quite average socioeconomic status. It is also shown that most adoptors were contacted by Program extension workers. Second, evidence is presented from a study of adoptions in various districts of India during 1966. The use of sterilization and the IUD is demonstrated to be significantly asssociated with variables measuring the amount of Program inputs in any district.

The objective of planners is not just to make a positive return for the nation on the resources that are invested. They also aim to make as large a positive return as possible. Thus, it is important to know what constraints have operated to limit acceptance of family planning.

Fertility control implies that some means must be found to influence the decisions of millions of family units. Chapter VI presents a model of rational family behavior and suggests that, for family planning programs to be effective, they must attempt to change the value which parents attach to children and to raise the effective price that parents pay for the children they have. It is not enough to establish clinics and pass out information concerning the existence of contraception. On the basis of the discussion in Chapter VI, it is argued in Chapter VII that the major constraint limiting the expansion of the Program is the narrow conception of the possible approaches to the problem. Little has been done to change parents' motivations, and, as yet, the efforts to make child-bearing more expensive have not been very enthusiastic. Even within the existing approach, however, administration has been a major constraint.

Chapter VIII presents a history of the attitude of economic planners in India to the programs of fertility control. It is argued that until very recently they did not pay sufficient attention to the economic potential of fertility control. Fortunately, this attitude seems to have changed during recent years.

There are a number of underlying themes that run throughout the study. First of all there is our prejudice that it is better to make some estimate of the impact of a major Program of social reform, even when the necessary data is of very low quality, than it is to ignore evaluation. Without systematic efforts at evaluation it is unlikely that program administrators will ever appreciate either their successes or their failures until it is too late to make use of the information for improved decision making. Ignorance is very unlikely to prompt improvement. Evaluation is primarily a tool to improve the decisions that are made by responsible administrators. A second and closely related theme is that evaluation improves as the quality of the data on which it is based improves. An evaluation based on poor data may be better than none, but the potential improvement in decision making that can result from improved data is more than enough to justify the high cost involved. Another theme which receives constant attention is that in evaluating the effect of government programs such as family planning it is very important to treat the causal influence of government directly. In other words it is important to take the role of evaluation seriously and to treat the impact of the government's activities in the broadest social context.

Any reader who has read this far into the introduction will recognize that this study ranges over too wide a field to provide adequate treatment for all topics. My aim has not been to present a complete evaluation of all aspects of the Indian Family Planning Program. Such a task is much better left to a group such as the Evaluation Team sent out by the United Nations or the World Bank. They have many more resources with which to work and they come to the problem with greater authority and experience. My purpose has been, rather, to discuss some aspects of the problem that seemed to have been neglected at the time I began my research.

Because the dimensions of the topic are so large, I have been obliged to limit my treatment of birth prevention to contraception in the narrowest of senses. Thus, I have not dealt with either the important question of age at marriage or the problem of abortion in anything like the depth that their importance merits. There are other issues that are also slighted.* For example, I have not discussed the complex set of relationships among the various organizations that are involved in the process of allocating resources to the Family Planning Program. Some day I would like to deal with them all more completely.

Much of the material for this study was collected during our eleven month stay in India during 1966 and 1967. The rich but incomplete published literature and personal discussion with more recent visitors to India has been the source of observations relating to the last three years. Naturally, the dependence upon sources available in the United States limits the accuracy and relevance of some of the conclusions.

---

* Since this study went to press an important official report concerning the Indian Family Planning Program has appeared. (Government of India, Planning Commission, Program Evaluation Organization, *Family Planning in India: An Evaluation*, Delhi, 1970.) In conjunction with the U.N. reports and the studies listed in the first footnote of Chapter Four, it should be a good source for the reader who wishes information beyond the scope of the present study.

Acknowledgments

I HAVE SPENT a long time working on this study and many people have helped me see it to completion.

I am especially grateful to my dissertation committee at the University of California, Berkeley; Professors Kingsley Davis, Benjamin Ward, and Van Dusen Kennedy. Their comments have made it a much better study than it would have been if I had done it alone. Professor Davis, especially, has gone out of his way to make the kind of critical comment upon which I was able to build improvements.

I had a Fulbright scholarship during the year I spent in India, and I am thankful for the experience. While in India, I worked at the Institute of Economic Growth under the general supervision of Dr. S. N. Agarwala, whose influence upon my thinking should be evident in the footnotes. Other members of the Institute staff who were very helpful to me during my stay are Professors P. N. Dhar and A. M. Khusro, Dr. Ashish Bose, Dr. J. N. Sinha, Mr. P. B. Desai, and Mr. R. P. Goyal. Peter King of the Ford Foundation staff in New Delhi made many useful suggestions in the early stages of my work.

During the past year I have made many revisions and improvements. My colleagues at The University of Michigan Center for Population Planning—Professors Jason Finkle, John Takeshita, Tom Poffenberger, Fred Munson, S. Kar and Leslie Corsa have made useful suggestions and provided a challenging academic environment. Other members of the

Center—David Kleinman, Rene Cabrera, Pierre Pradervand, Steve Thomas and Gene Weiss, have also made valuable contributions. I also want to thank Professor Ronald Freedman for his help and encouragement.

I would also like to thank my research assistants. Miss Stephany Reineck and Mrs. Judy Coakley helped many parts of the revision. Jack Goodman did yeoman service with the revision of the tables and other materials. Mrs. Kristina Stevens typed the final drafts of the manuscript.

My work during the year was supported by the 211D institutional grant from USAID. That organization is of course not responsible for the results.

Ruth Simmons is the shadow author. The mistakes are my own.

CHAPTER ONE

Investments In Family Planning

THE INDIAN Family Planning Program is one of the many programs for economic and social development that have been introduced by the government of India in the hope of improving the lot of the Indian people. The Family Planning Program attempts to prevent births by providing advice and services at government health centers, by employing mass media and extension services to inform the population of the existence of the program and to convince them of the need to limit family size, and by providing research and other facilities needed to complete the program. A total of Rs. 280 million were spent on family planning during the first three five year plans, and Rs. 3,000 million have been allotted to the Program for the Fourth Five Year Plan.[1] By thus devoting resources to the Program, the government of India hopes to reduce the rate of growth of the population and to improve the well-being of those people who will make up the population of India in future years.

The resources employed by the Family Planning Program could have been devoted to other ends. The doctors could spend their energies curing the ill, vehicles could be used to meet the demand for transportation in other sectors, and

1

buildings could be used as schools and warehouses rather than as clinics. By devoting current resources to the attainment of future ends, the Family Planning Program constitutes an investment in exactly the same sense that the construction of a steel mill or a textile factory is an investment.

The main purpose of the present study is to look at the Family Planning Program in India as an investment and to assess its impact according to the principles postulated by investment theory. In doing so, we will have to address ourselves to the following questions: What are the returns to the nation from investments in family planning? What are the costs involved? Have the expenditures made to date been justifiably spent, on economic grounds, or would the resources have been more advantageously applied to other opportunities? Has the Program been expanded as far as it should be, or is there a persuasive case for using even more resources for family planning investments? Do economic criteria of success provide a method for allocating resources with the Family Planning Program?

THE ALLOCATION OF RESOURCES AMONG INVESTMENT OPPORTUNITIES

The main objective of economic planning in India is to use the nation's resources "rationally" to achieve certain stated national goals. By "rationally" we mean that one seeks to accomplish any given objective with a minimum of resources, or, conversely, to accomplish a maximum of ends with a given quantity of resources. The principal responsibility for resource allocation in India lies with the Planning Commission. In the most general (and inoperable) terms, the principles to be followed for the best use of resources are clear. Once the total amount of resources to be invested has been decided, the budget should be spent in such a manner that no other allocation pattern would lead to greater benefits for the nation. Another way of expressing the same idea is to say that the marginal rate of return for all investments must be the same. If it is not the same, the total return can be increased by shifting resources from the low-return investments to the high-return investments. The problem is, of course, to decide what constitutes a benefit in the Indian context, and to relate particular investment allocations to the benefits.

Before discussion the problem of analyzing investments in family planning in detail, it may be useful to examine investment decisions in a more familiar context.[2] Suppose the Planning Commission wants to know the value of withdrawing resources from current use and devoting them to the construction of a foundry. Suppose, furthermore, there is agreement that the only objective of national planning is to raise national income and, consequently, the Planning Commission measures the value of an investment in terms of the investment's contribution to national income.[3] Now, assume that there is no uncertainty concerning either the prices of inputs or outputs or the amount of output that can be produced and sold. Finally, assume that prices of both inputs and outputs are competitive and therefore reflect the full utility of resources in other uses. The resources are devoted to the construction of a piece of capital—a building and the auxiliary equipment—which will, in combination with labor, raw materials, and management services, permit the production in future years of castings which could not be produced otherwise.

The cost of investment can be measured by the market value of the resources used. The return will be distributed over a number of years. In each future year it is the difference between the total revenue of the firm (i.e. the number of units of output multiplied by the price of each unit) and the variable costs (i.e. the cost of labor, raw materials, and management services used). We are assuming that all of the goods in question are correctly valued by their market prices. That is, if we use the market wage in the process of valuation, we are implying that the wage reflects the real scarcity of labor—an assumption that economists often choose to modify. Given our assumptions, the economists of the Planning Commission are left with two sets of information. First, they know the cost of the investment in the initial year (or years) and, second, they know the expected set of returns for each year in the future that the project is expected to operate. Some method must be found for dealing with the time element since it is clear that a unit of income five years from now is not the same thing as a unit of income in the present. The usual way around this problem is to discount the returns from the investment to the present, using the socially "correct" interest rate.[4] Then, the value of the investment can be represented by the following formula:

$$\text{Present value of investment in Year } 0 = \sum_{t=0}^{n} \frac{B_t}{(1+i)^t} - C_0$$

where: i = discount rate
   B_t = benefit in year t minus variable costs in year t
   C_0 = initial cost
   t = number of years elapsed since base year (t=0)
   n = life expectancy of investment

The present value of an investment represents, then, the amount of money that an entrepreneur should be willing to pay for the opportunity to invest in the foundry. It also represents the return to the nation—the discounted net addition to material income that results from the construction of this piece of capital.

The above discussion avoids issues that complicate many investment decisions.[5] First, there is more difficulty in establishing a set of relevant prices than the above discussion implies. Labor services in India are often said to be overvalued by the market wage rate. That is to say, the prevailing prices of either the inputs or the outputs may not reflect their scarcity. As a consequence, the problem of choosing the relevant set of prices becomes a very important part of the decision-making process. The choice of a proper discount rate is a case in point. A second problem, not mentioned in the above discussion, is that there are uncertainties inherent in any investment program. For example, a future change in prices may invalidate all of the current calculations. Third, there are often costs or benefits transmitted from one decision to another outside of the market. The foundry, for example, might be a major source of air pollution, thus creating costs for other economic units. The foundry which creates the pollution problem is never (or seldom) held responsible for the pollution that it creates. Finally, determining the optimal scale of an investment is as important as determining the return to an investment of specified size.

INVESTMENTS IN FAMILY PLANNING

In principle, the problem of assessing the value of a specific investment in family planning is not very different from the example given above. As in the case of the foundry, we need only to establish the number of units of output in each future year and the value of the output to make a correct valuation of the output stream of the program. In fact, however, in the case of the Family Planning Program, both the choice of an appropriate value per unit of output and the determination of the output (i.e. prevented births) are profoundly difficult. These problems will be discussed at great length in later chapters. Here, it is important only to put them in perspective.

In the case of the foundry, the market price is satisfactory —at least as a preliminary estimate of the value of a unit of output. It is more complicated to estimate the value of a birth prevented. Clearly, if there are ten or a million fewer births in 1969 than there would have been in the absence of the Family Planning Program, the changed circumstances will have some sort of enduring effect on the economy. The missing people will not consume and they will not produce.

The rest of the population thus gains the goods and services they would have used and loses the productive contribution they would have made. We will discuss the problem of evaluating the changes caused by preventing births in Chapter II, where a number of alternative estimates of the value of preventing a birth are derived from some models relating population size to economic aggregates.

The problem of determining the number of births prevented by a family planning program is also very complex. Analytically, the problem can be seen in two steps. The first step is to identify the changes in behavior that result from the existence of the program. Who are the people that have been reached by the program, and exactly how has that part of their behavior which determines the probability of a birth been affected? The most obvious kind of behavioral changes that would concern us would be changes in the use of contraception[6] (i.e. the adoption of a method of birth control for the first time or the change from one method to another), but changes in the family's attitudes toward family size and other less readily identifiable changes would also be relevant. Once we have identified the behavioral changes, it is necessary to translate these changes into the number of births prevented. This translation involves assumptions concerning fertility performance in the absence of the behavioral changes caused by the program. The number of births prevented is the final measure of output of the program; but it is much more difficult to establish the connection between the inputs of the Family Planning Program and the output of births prevented than it is to make the connection between the inputs in the process of producing castings and the output of castings. The problem of estimating the number of births prevented from past family planning activities is discussed in Chapter III, and further discussion of the causal inferences concerning the relationship between the government Family Planning Program and final output is included in Chapters IV, V, and VI.

In the above discussion we have been assuming that the investment in family planning that we are considering is of a specified size and nature—that is to say, we know the total amount of expenditure that has been authorized and how it is to be allocated. Such an assumption is meaningful if we are considering (as we will be) past investments. The investments made in past years in family planning are part of the historical record, and at least the size of the input has been determined by events. The outputs, on the other hand, may vary. Much of the discussion in the next chapters will be devoted to a consideration of the economic implications of these past investments. It is important that we know whether the return on such projects justifies the amount expended. Such a retrospective study, however, does not exhaust the area for analysis. Perhaps even more important than knowing the return from past investments is knowing the possible return from future expenditures. When we consider the future, it is no longer possible to assume that the size of the investment package remains constant. Instead, we must make such comments as we can upon the ideal size of the Program. This we will attempt in Chapter VII. In other words, the following analysis can be divided into two parts. First, we ask whether past expeditures have had a positive economic return. Then, having found that the return was positive (to anticipate), we turn to the question of whether the return was as large as possible—an optimal investment.

WHY BOTHER?

The approach to the Indian Family Planning Program outlined in the previous section is quite complicated and, before asking anyone to read further, it might be well to say a few words about the worthiness of the enterprise. What is the contribution that this study seeks to make, and how does the approach to family planning outlined in the following pages differ from that of authorities in the field?

The most obvious difference between the present study and other studies[7] of the Indian Family Planning Program is that in this study the primary focus is upon the economic consequences of the Program. An attempt is made to keep constantly in mind the questions: How much of a contribution is this program making toward the national development goals set out in the national Five Year Plans? How much of a contribution could the Program make under optimal circumstances?

Many authorities concerned with the evaluation of the Indian Family Planning Program or with family planning programs in general have pointed out that the conclusions that are reached depend very much upon the perspective from which one views the Program. Even in an overview, there are several alternative approaches. For example, there are at least three levels on which the Indian government tends to view the Family Planning Program. The first, which is that adopted here, is illustrated by the statement in the Third Five Year Plan document that the Family Planning Program is at the "very heart of planned development." Economic planners will thus wish to evaluate the Program from the point of view of its contribution to planned development.

On the second level, the actual administrators of the Program tend to view "a reduction in the birth rate" as the "main goal."[8] In their terms, the principal measures of program effectiveness must be any "change in the birth rate." Changes in the birth rate are presumably chosen as a measure of program effectiveness because they reflect the demographic impact of the official family planning activities; but there are obvious difficulties with using this measure. To begin with, the birth rate may fluctuate for reasons unconnected with the program. Second, in India, since the vital statistics are unreliable, we do not really know what the birth rate is at any given time. Consequently, we are obliged to use other, usually indirect, measures of demographic impact. These are difficult problems, but we cannot avoid them since some quantitative measure of demographic impact is a necessary part of the larger attempt to place the Program in the context of economic planning goals. In the following pages, we will make some considerable effort to evaluate the demographic impact of the Program, but these efforts are part of the larger attempt to place the Program in the context of economic planning goals.

A third view of the Family Planning Program is in terms of the "operational goals" set up by administrators. They are

> to create for 90 per cent of the married adult population of India, the three basic conditions needed for accelerating the adoption of family planning by couples: group acceptance, knowledge about family planning, and available supplies.[9]

In terms of this third set of goals, success would be measured by such indicators as the percentage of the population who knows about family planning and the possible sources of information and supplies, the extent to which couples in India are willing to accept a "small family norm" for themselves, and other similar indicators. Clearly, the extent to which these operational goals are achieved has a bearing on the success of the Program, and this fact should not be ignored. However, these goals are not complete in and of themselves any more than is the goal of reducing the birth rate. Both sets of goals must be related to the larger development goals in order to be complete.

We do not mean to imply by the above remarks that internal efforts to evaluate the program have no meaning nor importance. As we shall see later, there is a very close connection between the main internal goal of the Program (birth rate reduction) and the size of the economic benefits generated by the Program. Thus, in a sense, close attention to the extent to which the birth rate is affected by the Program will give, in many ways, a measure of Program success similar to that achieved by using the goals of economic planning as criteria. Moreover, internal evaluations of the family planning effort are a very important part of our own effort. If we know how effective the Program has been in preventing births, then it is not difficult to conclude something about how effective it is in terms of its contribution to the goals of economic planning. Likewise, knowledge of the number of contraceptive users and of changes in public attitudes toward family planning may make it easier to determine the probable effect of the Program on the birth rate. In other words, we will attempt to use other studies of the Indian Family Planning Program in an effort to place it in the proper context of economic planning. We do so at the risk of adding nothing new to the knowledge of those people who are laboring to find the most efficient way to decrease the birth rate or to accomplish the operational goals of the program. For these groups, however, this study will have the advantage of adding a new perspective to material already familiar and of presenting some new analyses developed to fill in the chinks in the information presently available.

In a more important sense, the study is addressed to an audience of economists. There is a tendency for our profession, as well as others, to avoid dealing with problems that have been claimed decisively by other professional groups as their domain. Thus, in the case at hand, most economists, while recognizing that family planning programs have an economic impact, prefer to relegate the conduct and evaluation of such programs to demographers and public health specialists. Some economists have made important contributions to demographic analysis, but their work has remained in large measure outside of the mainstream of modern economics. This study attempts to make clear the past and potential future contribution of the Family Planning Program to economic development in India. The hope is that by making such an analysis, our understanding of optimal resource allocation for economic planning can be improved.

ECONOMIC RESEARCH ON
FAMILY PLANNING IN INDIA[10]

A number of economists have concerned themselves with the question of family planning in India. The first, and perhaps the best, study is the one done by Coale and Hoover in which they attempted to describe the connection between population growth and the process of economic development in India.[11] They did so in such a way as to make absolutely clear the advantages of population limitation. Their research was conducted before the Indian Family Planning Program really got under way, however, and there is no attempt at an actual evaluation of the Program. Stephen Enke has written a number of articles attempting to determine the value of preventing a birth.[12] Enke's work, like that of Coale and Hoover, has been pioneering but his efforts have not been carried to the point of actually looking at the Indian Program. Rather, they have been concerned with the important overall problem of making clear the large return from the prevention of a birth. Myrdal's observations on the economic aspects of the Indian Family Planning Program are contained in the relevant chapters in his massive work on Asian economic development.[13] The framework he uses, however, is quite different from that employed here. His emphasis is on the general social context in which the Program exists, and there is no effort to evaluate the economic contribution of past accomplishments or to explicitly assess the Program's implications for planning. In the next chapter we will compare the relevant results from this previous research to our own findings. More recently Gunnar Myrdal and Julian Simon[14] have commented on the work of Enke and of Coale and Hoover. Simon's comments are directed towards improving the estimate of the value of preventing a birth.

NOTES

1. India, Planning Commission, *Fourth Five Year Plan 1969–74: Draft*, New Delhi, p. 312.
2. There is considerable literature on the subject of optimal investment decisions. One good discussion is in Roland N. McKean, *Public Spending* (New York: McGraw-Hill, 1968). Another is Otto Eckstein, "A Survey of the Theory of Public Expenditure Criteria," in *Public Finances: Needs, Sources, and Utilization*, ed. by J. M. Buchanan (Princeton, N.J.: Princeton University Press, 1961), pp. 439–494. Also S. A. Marglin, *Public Investment Criteria: Benefit-Cost Analysis for Planned Economic Growth* (London: George Allen & Unwin, Ltd., 1967), and Richard A. Musgrave, "Cost-Benefit Analysis and the Theory of Public Finance," *Journal of Economic Literature*, 7 (Sept. 1969), pp. 797–806.
3. Note that other objectives for national planning are possible, and the relationships among alternative goals is an important part of the discussion in Chapter II.
4. There is much debate in the literature on this subject. It is discussed in Eckstein, "Theory of Public Expenditure Criteria," and in the commentary on Eckstein's paper by J. Hirschleifer, "Comments," in *Public Finances*, ed. Buchanan, pp. 495–501.
5. The literature on the complications in investment theory discussed here is huge. Reasonably complete references are given in McKean, *Public Spending*, or in A. R. Prest and R. Turvey, "Cost-Benefit Analysis: A Survey," *Economic Journal*, 75 (December 1965), pp. 683–735.
6. The term "contraception" as used here is not restricted to mechanical methods. Other approaches such as the rhythm method, abstinence, or coitus interruptus have a similar effect. We will not discuss the problem of changes in the age of marriage in the following chapters, but to the extent that such changes result from the program influence, their contribution is as significant as those resulting from contraception. For any given couple, changes in the age of marriage are likely to be a superior method of preventing births, since it "prevents" births earlier, by definition, than does contraception within marriage. Abortion and infanticide are also topics given scant attention here, although both are relevant to any comprehensive discussion of the topic.

7. By "other studies" we mean reports like that of the United Nations, Commissioner for Technical Assistance, Department of Economic and Social Affairs, *Report on the Family Planning Programme in India* (New York, February 1966) and *An Evaluation of the Family Planning Programme of the Government of India* (New York, November 1969); the internal reports of the Family Planning Program such as those included in the Agendas of the Family Planning Council meetings; and the periodic review articles by people associated with the Program as, for example, the article by B. L. Raina, "India" in *Family Planning and Population Programs,* edited by Bernard Berelson (Chicago: The University of Chicago Press, 1966), pp. 111–121, and similar reviews such as these published in *Studies in Family Planning.* There are also articles on the problems of evaluating the progress of programs (such as those in India), as, for example, S. N. Agarwala, "Evaulating the Effectiveness of a Family Planning Programme," in *Research in Family Planning,* edited by C. Kiser (Princeton, N. J.: Princeton University Press, 1961), pp. 409–421; and C. Chandrasekaran and M. W. Freyman, "Evaluating Community Family Planning Programs," in *Public Health and Population Change: Current Research Issues,* edited by M. C. Sheps and J. C. Ridley (Pittsburgh: University of Pittsburgh Press, 1965), pp. 266–286.

8. B. L. Raina, *Family Planning Programme, Report for 1962–63,* Director General, Health Services, Ministry of Health, New Delhi, 1964, p. 44.

9. Raina, *Family Planning Programme, Report for 1962–63,* p. 45.

10. A useful bibliography is K. B. Suri and S. P. Mohanty, "A Bibliography of Cost-Benefit Studies on Family Planning in India," Demographic Training and Research Center, *Newsletter,* No. 31 (Jan. 1970), pp. 3–10.

11. Ansley Coale and Edgar M. Hoover, *Population Growth and Economic Development in Low Income Countries* (Princeton, N.J.: Princeton University Press, 1958).

12. Stephen Enke, "The Economics of Government Payments to Limit Population," *Economic Development and Cultural Change,* 8 (July 1960), pp. 339–348; and "The Gains to India from Population Control: Some Money Measures and Incentive Schemes," *Review of Economics and Statistics,* 42 (May 1960), pp. 175–181.

13. Gunnar Myrdal, *Asian Drama* (New York: Pantheon, 1968), Vol. II, Chapters 27 and 28; Vol. III, Appendices 7 and 12.

14. Julian Simon, "The Value of Avoided Births to Underdeveloped Countries," *Population Studies,* 23, No. 1 (March 1969), pp. 61–68.

CHAPTER TWO

The Goals of Economic Planning and The Value of Preventing A Birth

ECONOMIC PLANNING has as its chief objective the increase in the welfare of the inhabitants of the country for which the planning is being done. The responsibility of government planners is to allocate the scarce resources under their control to assure the maximum possible level of welfare. Welfare is, however, a notoriously difficult concept to define or measure.[1] Consequently, planners and economists generally are obliged to resort to imperfect indices. The Indian government has listed a number of goals for economic planning. It is appropriate that we couch our discussion of the returns from birth prevention in the context of the goals chosen by the responsible authorities in India. Value judgments are involved in any case, but there seems to be some virtue in using those of the responsible government authorities.[2] Thus, the present chapter attempts to assess the consequences of birth prevention for the goals of economic planning in India.

A word of caution is appropriate at this point. The consequences we are discussing will result when a birth is prevented whether or not that act of prevention results from government investments in family planning. The value of a birth prevented is analogous to the price of output in more conventional economic analysis. But an output can have a price independent of where it is produced. To assess the economic consequences of investments in family planning, it is necessary to make some inferences concerning the number of births that can be said to have been prevented by the activities of the government. Such inferences can be combined with estimates of the value of a birth prevented to give an estimate of the total return to the investment. In this chapter we are only concerned with estimating the value of a birth prevented.

The Indian Five Year Plans list the objectives of planned development as an increase in the national income and the level of living, rapid industrialization, freedom from the need to import food, expansion of employment opportunities, and the reduction of inequalities in wealth and income.[3] As the Indian planners recognize, these goals are interrelated. For example, both a higher national income and an increased number of job opportunities will result from a program of industrialization, but heavy emphasis on industrial investment may maximize neither employment nor income. As a second example, distributional factors affect the rate of growth of national income and are, in turn, partially the result of the rate of growth and the form which growth takes. Another instance, more relevant here, is that when government policy affects the size of the population, policies which maximize total national income may not maximize per capita income, ie., the standard of living.[4]

As a consequence of the essential interrelation of economic goals, planners must define carefully the aims of policy and establish some criterion for choosing among conflicting goals. The Indian planners have placed the greatest emphasis on increasing national income and income per capita. It would probably be fair to say that for most purposes they treated these two objectives as synonymous. On the other hand, when policies have had conflicting potential effects on income and one of the other goals (e.g., employment or income distribution), the former has usually been given preference. In those situations where there was no conflict among the goals of planning, planners in India have tried to create policies which would have a favorable effect on each of the goals. The demographic change which results from birth prevention affects all of the planning objectives. For this reason we will discuss the effects of demographic variables on the economy under the headings of the objectives of Indian planning.

These objectives can be put into two categories. The first, national income and the standard of living, is composed of goals which are easily quantified and incorporated into simple models of income determination. The second, including rapid industrialization, the creation of employment opportunities and the reduction of inequalities of wealth and income, is composed of objectives which are more difficult to incorporate into formal models designed to assess the impact of family planning programs. Moreover, there is every reason to think that the second set of goals overlap with the first set of goals (i.e., a larger national income may lead to higher employment). There is, however, no formal statement on the part of the Indian planning authorities as to what relative weights they would attach to each category. Consequently, even if we could construct a formal model including all five of the listed goals, it does not follow that we would have a clear, normative framework in which to evaluate the consequences of the Family Planning Program. The approach adopted here is to measure the value of family planning activities in terms of the first group of national planning goals. Subsequently, we show that the Family Planning Program yields positive returns in terms of all of the other goals. Thus, if the second group of goals is given a weight (positive), then the returns from the program are understated when measured only in terms of national income and the standard of living.

ECONOMIC BENEFITS OF PREVENTING A BIRTH AS MEASURED BY THE GOALS OF NATIONAL INCOME AND PER CAPITA NATIONAL INCOME[5]

The economic benefits which result from government programs to reduce the number of births taking place are difficult to evaluate. The estimate of the benefits differs according to the measure of welfare employed and the complexity of the relationship between economic and demographic variables which is postulated in the estimating procedure.

It should be noted that there is little agreement on the causes of economic growth in general and even less on the role demographic patterns play in the process.[6] Some consensus might be established on the idea that the nature and magnitude of the stock of physical capital plays a role in determining the level of output that a nation can sustain and that changes in the capital stock are an important determinant of the rate of growth of national output. On the other hand, considerable debate would arise as soon as efforts were made to define the dimensions of capital's influence and the mechanism through which it operates. Labor is another factor of accepted importance. The sheer number of human beings available to do productive work is a major determinant of economic growth. Perhaps even more important is the quality of the labor force—its health, level of training and motivation—and the manner in which it is organized and combined with capital. A final factor closely related to this last factor is the level of technology which is being applied. Changes in the level of technology as changes in the other variables can make an important contribution to economic growth.

Our objective in this section is to estimate the impact of fertility reduction on economic growth. The task would be relatively easy if we had agreement on the causes and mechanisms leading to growth and upon the role population growth plays in the process. Since we do not have this agreement, we are obliged to resort to an examination of a range of possibilities. We will discuss some possibilities in terms of increasing complexity. The numbers which we derive are not by themselves an indication of the return from investments in population control, since they are not related to the costs or to the outputs of any specific program. In later chapters the estimate of the value of preventing a birth will be used to compare the costs of Indian investments in family planning with the benefits, but the results of this chapter are only a beginning of the analysis.

The basic procedure used to estimate the value of preventing a birth is an analysis of the economic consequences of two different population projections. The difference of a million births in the base year which distinguishes the projections may have a variety of economic consequences, depending on the nature of the relationship between population size and age structure and the national economy. But all of the estimates presented in this chapter take the two basic projections as their point of departure.

The high population projection is constructed by applying the anticipated growth rates as proposed in the Fourth Five Year Plan Draft of 1969. From the base year 1967–68 estimate of 514 million, the population is projected forward at an annual growth rate of 2.5 percent through 1973–74. After 1973–74 the growth rate decreases linearly until, in 1980–81, it reaches 1.7. During the following decade the rate of growth decreases further until in 1990–91 it reaches 1.2 percent per year. The low population projection assumes that there were one million fewer births in 1968–69 than occurred under the high-population assumption. As a result, the high-population estimate exceeds the low population estimate by the number of survivors from the extra births in 1968–69.[7]

No adjustment has been made for the second-generation births that would take place in the higher population as it reaches marriage age. The two population projections are given in Table II-1. In the following pages we discuss the economic consequences of these differing population projections, according to three different examples of how population and economic variables can be thought to interact.

EXAMPLE I

The simplest situation is where the time path of national income is independent of the size of the population. The total output of the economy is affected neither by changes in the size of the labor force nor by demographically caused alterations in the amount of investment. Consider two possible states of the world. In the first situation (low population—"L"), the government has used a certain amount of resources in year one (1967–68) to "prevent" one million births in year two (1968–69). In the second situation (high population—"H") these expenditures have not been undertaken.

To evaluate the impact of population growth on the goals of national planning, it is necessary to have some projection of the future path of national income growth. The projection used for Example I is presented in Table II-1, Column 3. The basic economic data have been taken from the plan documents where possible, or are based on a reasonable assessment of past performance. The rate of economic growth approximates that projected by the Draft Outline of the Fourth Five Year Plan.[8]

What are the benefits from the birth prevention program? Measured by the criterion of national income, the benefits would be determined by the difference between the size of the national income associated with the high-population projection and that associated with the low-population projection.

Benefit $(t) = Y_{Lt} - Y_{Ht}$
where:

t = the year
Y = national income
P = population
L,H = subscripts for the high- and low-population situation

In this example there are no benefits since, by assumption, the growth of aggregate income is not different in the two situations.

If we measure the benefits in terms of per capita income, then the benefits are very large and can be measured by the amount of additional income that would be required in each future year to equate the per capita income of the low-population situation with that of the high-population situation.

Benefits $(t) = (Y_t/P_{Lt} - Y_t/P_{Ht}) \cdot P_{Ht}$

Using this criterion, the present value (calculated at 10 percent) of preventing a single birth, Rs. 5311, is about 9.8 times the per capita income of India in 1967–68. Table II-2 shows the present value of preventing a birth for the different criteria according to each example.

Continuing this example, if total consumption is the criterion, there is no benefit from birth prevention, since the aggregate amount of consumption does not vary. But if per capita consumption is the criterion, then the benefit to the economy can be measured by the cost of raising the consumption per capita in the high-population situation to that in the low-population situation.

TABLE II-1

DATA FOR THE CALCULATION OF THE VALUE OF PREVENTING A BIRTH—FOR EXAMPLE III.

Order (1)	Fiscal Year[a] (2)	Population (in millions)		National Income (in millions of rupees)		Income Per Capita (in rupees)	
		High Estimate (3)	Low Estimate (4)	High Population (5)	Low Population (6)	High Population (7)	Low Population (8)
1	1967–68	514.000	514.000	279,300	279,300	543.39	543.39
2	1968–69	527.000	526.072	293,265	293,265	556.48	557.46
3	1969–70	540.000	539.162	308,273	308,298	570.88	571.81
4	1970–71	554.000	553.185	324,429	324,479	585.61	586.57
5	1971–72	567.000	566.205	341,820	341,898	602.86	603.84
6	1972–73	582.000	581.219	360,597	360,704	619.58	620.60
7	1973–74	596.000	595.230	380,844	380,983	639.00	640.06
8	1974–75	610.000	609.237	402,735	402,909	660.22	661.33
9	1975–76	623.000	622.243	426,436	426,648	684.49	685.66
10	1976–77	636.000	635.247	452,153	452,407	710.93	712.17
11	1977–78	649.000	648.249	480,088	480,388	739.74	741.05
12	1978–79	661.000	660.252	510,511	510,814	772.33	773.67
13	1979–80	673.000	672.255	543,603	543,957	807.73	809.15

14	1980–81	685.000	684.257	579,678	580,088	846.25	847.76
15	1981–82	696.000	695.260	619,092	619,506	889.50	891.04
16	1982–83	707.000	706.264	662,090	662,567	936.48	938.13
17	1983–84	718.000	717.268	709,090	709,635	987.59	989.36
18	1984–85	729.000	728.271	760,491	761,111	1043.20	1045.09
19	1985–86	739.000	738.275	816,733	817,435	1105.19	1107.22
20	1986–87	750.000	749.279	878,328	879,120	1171.10	1173.29
21	1987–88	760.000	759.282	945,866	946,674	1244.56	1246.80
22	1988–89	770.000	769.287	1,019,802	1,020,713	1324.42	1326.83
23	1989–90	779.000	778.291	1,100,859	1,101,882	1413.17	1415.77
24	1990–91	789.000	788.294	1,189,777	1,190,924	1507.96	1510.76
25	1991–92	798.000	797.298	1,287,315	1,288,598	1613.18	1616.21
26	1992–93	808.000	807.302	1,394,362	1,395,795	1725.70	1728.96

ª starts April 1.

TABLE II-2

THE VALUE OF PREVENTING A BIRTH
(RUPEES—1967–68 PRICES)

Example	Criterion			
	Y	Y/P	C	C/P
Discount Rate = 5%				
I	0	8,957	0	7,514
II	6,478	15,442	4,218	11,736
III	5,264	14,228	3,295	10,813
Discount Rate = 10%				
I	0	5,311	0	4,500
II	2,976	8,290	1,798	6,300
III	2,486	7,800	1,426	5,928
Discount Rate = 15%				
I	0	3,564	0	3,045
II	1,527	5,092	825	3,870
III	1,314	4,880	663	3,709

Parameters Used: $Y_0 = 27930.0$ crore rupees, $P_0 = 517$ million persons, $s = 0.12$, $x = 0.24$, $B = 2.4$.

$$\text{Benefit } (t) = (C_t/P_{Lt}) - C_t/P_{Ht}) \cdot P_{Ht}$$
$$\text{where: } C = \text{aggregate consumption}$$

By the per capita consumption criterion, the present value of the stream of benefits from preventing a birth is Rs. 4,500.

EXAMPLE II

The above measure assumes that national income growth rates are not affected by the rate of growth or size of the national population. Following Demeny and Coale and Hoover[9] we can relax that assumption by making the rate of investment a function of per capita income, and national income a function of investment. The model we are discussing is of a very simple nature. Saving is automatically assumed to equal net investment (the rate of capital formation), and the sole determinant of the size of national income is the amount of capital existing in the system. Population is thus an intermediate variable making its influence felt through the rate of capital formation. Such factors as the rate of technological progress and the size of the labor force are not taken into account. The basic behavioral concept underlying the postulated relationship is that when per capita incomes go up, there will be a greater willingness and ability to save.[10] Such a change in the propensity to save is assumed to take place either because of higher personal savings or because the government is able to devote more of its resources to productive investments. The resulting change in income from year to year is described in the following equation.

$$Y_{t+1} = Y_t + P_t \left[\frac{s \dfrac{Y_0}{P_0} + x \left(\dfrac{Y_t}{P_t} - \dfrac{Y_0}{P_0} \right)}{B} \right],$$

where: s = rate of saving from per capita income in the initial period

x = marginal rate of saving out of per capita income

B = capital/output ratio

Y_0/P_0 = per capita income in the initial year

When we know the values of all the parameters and of two alternative growth paths for the national population, we can calculate the alternative growth paths for national income. Then, if we apply the aggregate income criterion of economic well-being to the two alternative situations, the benefits of a population control program are measured by:

$$\text{Benefit } (t) = Y_{Lt} - Y_{Ht}; \quad \text{Benefit } (t) = C_{Lt} - C_{Ht}$$

The per capita criteria become:

$$\text{Benefit } (t) = (Y_{Lt}/P_{Lt} - Y_{Ht}/P_{Ht}) \cdot P_{Ht}$$
$$\text{and Benefit } (t) = (C_{Lt}/P_{Lt} - C_{Ht}/P_{Ht}) \cdot P_{Ht}$$

Using the framework suggested above, we again compare two situations. In the first the population is growing according to the projection described for the high population in Example I; in the second, one million births are assumed to have been prevented and the total population is lower by the number of survivors of these million births.

In this case, the present value of preventing a single birth is Rs. 2,976 by the aggregate income criterion, and Rs. 8,290 by the per capita income criterion. The analogous figures for the consumption criteria are Rs. 1,798 and Rs. 6,300. The discount rate employed in making these estimates was 10 percent and only the first 25 years have been considered. These benefits are huge; the higher present value indicates that the benefits from preventing a birth are as much as fifteen times the per capita income of the base year. With a lower rate of interest or a longer time period, the benefits would be even greater.

EXAMPLE III: POPULATION GROWTH AFFECTS BOTH SAVING AND THE SIZE OF THE LABOR FORCE

The above results are changed if we assume that population affects income, not only through saving, but also through the labor services rendered.

It is often argued that population growth is beneficial because it increases the size of the labor force. This argument has little application to India, but in order to demonstrate exactly how little impact it has, Example II can be adjusted to take into account the additional labor services that will be associated with the higher population projection.

$$Y_{t+1} = Y_t + P_t \left[\frac{s \dfrac{Y_0}{P_0} + x \left(\dfrac{Y_t}{P_t} - \dfrac{Y_0}{P_0} \right)}{B} \right]$$

$$+ r_{t+1} \cdot X_{t+1} \cdot MVP_{t+1} - r_t \cdot X_t \cdot MVP_t$$

The income associated with the higher population projection is calculated according to the above formula, where the extra terms appended to the equation add the marginal contribution resulting from the extra labor services. In this case, r_t is the labor force participation rate, which has been assigned the following values, using 1961 census information as a rough guide.

$$r_{0\text{-}11} = 0.0$$
$$r_{12\text{-}14} = .30$$
$$r_{15\text{-}20} = .50$$
$$r_{21\text{-}25} = .73$$

X_t is calculated as the difference between the two population projections. MVP_t is the value product of a marginal worker. The average value product of labor (AVP) in 1961 was approximately 1,110 1967–68 rupees. Making the fairly safe assumption of marked diminishing marginal product of labor in India, the estimated MVP_t values are:[11]

$$MVP_{12\text{-}14} = 0.19 \; AVP = 210 \; Rs.$$
$$MVP_{15\text{-}20} = 0.25 \; AVP = 280 \; Rs.$$
$$MVP_{21\text{-}25} = 0.32 \; AVP = 350 \; Rs.$$

Thus, we have assumed that a marginal worker between the ages of twelve and fourteen will produce a fifth of the average value product produced by workers of all ages. The resulting estimate of the contribution of extra labor is probably on the high side of reality. The income stream associated with the low-population projection is calculated as in the basic equation of Example II, and the benefits are calculated as in Example II. Perhaps the most interesting result of this exercise is that the estimated value of preventing a birth is not changed very much by the additional complication. The principal reason why the introduction of labor services has a limited impact is that the productive contribution of the relevant cohort comes only after ten or twenty years, and with a reasonable discount rate, such delayed benefits do not carry much weight. Even the limited impact that we have built into Example III would be offset in the short run by lower fertility which is likely to permit increased participation from parents who have more time to work.

DISCUSSION

The three models of demographic-economic interaction are all relatively simple. Even Example III assumes that there are only two factors of production. There is no reference to the balance of payments, technological progress, entrepreneurship, the breakup of the economy into different sectors, or other factors which certainly play a role in determining the rate of economic growth. The examples do not represent an attempt to predict the rate of income growth for India. Rather, we are attempting to assess the consequences under ideal conditions of alternative patterns of population growth. Moreover, the values given in Table II-2 are, in a sense, average values. They do not take into account the differing contributions that might be made by different social classes, nor do they recognize that the value of preventing a birth will be different for the first birth prevented and for the ten millionth. In sum, then, the three examples given are based on a quite limited analysis of the relationship between population growth and the national economy.

One particular problem deserves special mention. Much of the recent literature on economic growth has pointed to the fact that only a small proportion of the growth in material output can be explained by the variations in the input of either capital or labor.[12] We do not yet know which factors best explain the residual.[13] But one major candidate has been improvements in the quality of the labor force. Such improvements are analogous to increases in the quantity of non-human resources, and, consequently, are known as human capital formation in the literature.[14] The impact of the higher population on human capital formation is probably basically similar to the impact of the larger population on investment as described in Example II. Proportionately more resources will be devoted to education as per capita incomes rise. Certainly, increasing expenditures on education are consistent with the cross-sectional and time-series evidence that we possess. Moreover, even with a fixed budget for education the existence of more children would mean less education for each, or, conversely, if more money is spent in an attempt to maintain average quality of education the money would have to be wthdrawn from alternative uses. In either case the higher population leads to a smaller total amount of capital formation.[15]

All of the estimates of the value of preventing a birth given in Table II-1 are based on a number of assumptions concerning the values to be given the parameters of the models involved. Perhaps the most important parameter is the base year per capita income. The figure used has been the per capita income of 1967–68 (Rs. 543). Similarly, the savings ratio, s, for the base year has been taken from official accounts to approximate 0.12 for 1967–68. The other parameters are more difficult to choose. For example, there is a great deal of controversy concerning the appropriate discount rate to be used. Thus, the estimates are given for three different rates. The favored incremental capital-output ratio (ICOR) of 2.4 has been chosen for two reasons. First, the Planning Commission suggested an ICOR of 2.4 for the first three Five Year Plans, and of 2.0 for the Fourth Five Year Plan. Second, the pramatic need for a growth rate in keeping with the Fourth Plan's anticipated growth rate of 5.5 percent implied that we would have to use an ICOR in this range. The Fourth Five Year Plan document anticipates a marginal rate of savings out of national income of 0.24. The equivalent rate out of per capita income is 0.36. This rate is probably unduly optimistic. We have somewhat arbitrarily chosen to use a figure of 0.24 as an estimate of the marginal rate of saving from per capita income. The high and low estimates of both the ICOR and marginal savings rate parameters represent reasonable limits on the range of parameter values.

To illustrate how these parameters affect the results, Table II-3 presents the value of preventing a birth under the per capita income criterion for Example III as calculated using several alternative marginal saving rates and capital-output ratios. It is clear that the results are sensitive to the parameters used, but the order of magnitude is consistently high for all combinations used. Thus, in the context of the analysis presented here, the value of preventing a birth is very large.

TABLE II-3

THE VALUE OF PREVENTING A BIRTH UNDER ALTERNATIVE ASSUMPTIONS CONCERNING THE CAPITAL–OUTPUT RATIO AND THE MARGINAL RATE OF SAVING—ACCORDING TO THE PER CAPITA INCOME CRITERION USING EXAMPLE III.

Marginal Rate of Saving from Per Capita Income	Capital-Output Ratio		
	2.0	2.4	3.0
.18	6,878	5,860	5.032
.24	9,869	7,800	6,242
.30	14,547	10,599	7,862

Figures are in 1967–68 rupees, with a 10 percent rate of discount.

It should be noted that the above procedures may understate the value of preventing a birth. First of all, the fact that the time span under consideration was restricted to twenty-five years certainly reduces to some extent the size of the benefits. Second, there has been no effort to take second-generation effects into account. Indian women marry early and begin to bear children before they are twenty. This second generation has economic consequences similar to, but delayed from, those of the first generation. Thus, preventing a birth in 1966 also helps to reduce the number of births in later decades. Finally, the criteria of national well-being employed in this discussion may themselves not represent the full value of preventing a birth. To the extent that other goals, say income distribution, are a concern above and beyond the size of per capita income, the deleterious effects of population growth on these goals should be added to the total measure of the benefits of preventing a birth. This last consideration will be discussed more fully in the next section.

THE EFFECTS OF BIRTH PREVENTION ON THE SECONDARY GOALS OF ECONOMIC PLANNING IN INDIA

Having discussed the value of preventing a birth according to the quantifiable aggregate income criteria in the section above, the analysis of the returns from preventing a single birth is completed by examining the additional returns which result from the effects of birth prevention on the secondary goals of economic planning. We will examine, in order, the probable effects of a successful birth-control program on the goals of a rapid industrialization, independence from foreign sources of food grains, full employment, and income equality.

Birth prevention has two kinds of effect on the possibility of *rapid industrialization*. First, as mentioned in our discussion of Example II, a higher rate of population growth may lead to less capital formation than would be possible with fewer births. In that case, there are fewer investible resources for industrial projects. Second, the demand for industrial products is likely to be lower in the high-population situation. One of the basic characteristics of demand is that people seek to have enough to eat first and only having satisfied that need do they begin to spend a larger part of their income on the products of organized industry. In India a very large portion of personal budgets is spent on basic agricultural products—food and fiber. An increase in population under these circumstances is likely to make demand more biased toward agricultural production than would the alternative increase in per capita income.[16] The same basic economic patterns that make birth prevention favorable to more rapid rates of industrialization make it more difficult for India to free itself of *the need to import food grains* in the situation with the higher populations.

Employment goals are also affected by population growth rates. Comparing the high- and low-population growth rates discussed in the previous section, it is clear that the total population in the relevant working age groups will eventually be larger in the higher population situation. The increase in the labor force size results only after the cohort has reached working age. In the short run, therefore, there will be no change in the employment situation, but in the long run the higher population will either add to overall unemployment or will lower the productivity of the work force.[17]

The final objective of Indian planning is an improved *distribution of income*. The subject has not been widely discussed in the literature,[18] but there is every indication that rapid population growth accentuates the inequalities that exist in the system. The poorer segments of the population earn their incomes through the sale of labor services, and the wealthier segments of the population tend to have a large share of income in the form of returns to capital and land. The high rate of population growth tends to keep the return on labor services low and the return on capital and land high.

We have argued in this section that all of the secondary goals of economic planning would be positively affected by the prevention of births. To the extent that the described effects have an independent value in the social welfare function, the estimates of the value of preventing a birth given in Table II-2 understate the true value. No effort will be made here to correct for the understatement. It is important to note, however, that even the high figures calculated in the previous section are, in some sense, an incomplete measure of the value of birth prevention.

Table II-2 presents not one value for preventing a birth, but twelve. How are we to choose among them? My own feeling is that Example III is probably the best version of the relationship between birth prevention and the national income, and it is my feeling that the whole thrust of the Planning Commission's published goals for national planning is that the single most appropriate objective function is per capita income.[19] Using Example III and the per capita income criterion the value of preventing a birth is Rs. 7,800. The value of preventing a birth which we have estimated is a marginal value. It may hold for, say, a twenty or thirty percent reduction in the level of fertility, but it does not hold indefinitely. Moreover, the value is specific to a particular base year. It is probably a reasonable approximation for a range of years around the base year, but it is less applicable to periods separated from the base year by a number of decades. In the following chapters we will apply the value of preventing a birth in 1967–68 to the estimation of the economic impact of the program in all years considered. It would be more appropriate to use a separate estimate (with prices held constant) for each year, but the extra precision is not worth the computational difficulties involved.

The policy implications of the figure are relatively clear. It represents the return to the prevention of a single birth. Thus, if it is possible to estimate the number of births prevented through past government efforts in the area of family planning, the total return to the Program can be estimated and compared with the expenditures on the Program. We will attempt such a comparison in Chapter IV. Perhaps more important, the responsible authorities can use the value of preventing a birth as the upper limit on the amount of money they can justify spending on preventing a single birth. The implication is that since the figure is so large, they can afford to spend a great deal of money, if necessary, without wasting the nation's resources.

A COMPARISON WITH OTHER STUDIES

Discussion of the costs of population growth or its inverse, the benefits of population control, has a long history. The two recent studies relevant to India are those of Coale and Hoover and Enke.[20] The focus of Coale and Hoover's book is the relationship between economic and demographic variables. After reviewing both the prevailing economic and demographic situations at the time their study was made, they construct a simulation of the possible economic implications of three different patterns of demographic growth. The simulation models focus on the impact of the different population growth patterns on capital formation and the supply of labor. Examples II and III belong to the same general family of models originated by Coale and Hoover. In these simulation exercises the demographic sector is seen as influencing the rates of capital formation and of growth of the labor force. The size of the capital stock and the labor supply at any given point in time determines the level of national income and of income per capita. Coale and Hoover use these models to illustrate the adverse economic effects of rapid population growth. Since family planning program evaluation is not a part of their research aim, they do not themselves derive the value of a birth prevented.

Enke's work has been more concerned with the normative economic implications of birth prevention. The principal aim of his early work was to indicate to policy makers the important advantages of fertility control.

In order to estimate the value of preventing a birth, Enke projected the consumption and the productive contribution of 1,000 births and discounted the two series to the year in which the births would have taken place. Because the consumption is much higher than any contribution of productive services during the first years after birth, the value of a birth is shown to be negative. Putting it in inverse form, the value of preventing a birth is positive and varies between two and five times per capita income, depending upon the exact assumptions that are made. The welfare criterion that Enke uses seems to be the per capita consumption of the population living at the time the birth is prevented. This criterion differs from the criteria used here. We have been assuming that the benefit is based on the entire population living at the time the benefit accrues. One of the principal reasons that our estimate of the benefits (using the per capita income criterion) is larger than those suggested by Enke is that we have assumed a relatively high rate of income growth. Enke's assumption that per capita production and consumption would remain constant at the initial levels over the period which he examines lowers the value of a birth prevented, but even after adjustments for the rate of growth, the benefit is larger than those suggested by Enke.

One further interjection should be made. The principal parties concerned with the birth of a child are the immediate family. For that family most births are a source of happiness. The happiness is by no means a simple function of the extra economic contribution which results from the child's presence. There are both economic and non-economic consequences resulting from a birth. As we have argued in the preceeding pages the net economic benefits derived from a birth are negative. Families have children despite the costs involved, and the main reason they undertake the many resulting obligations is that there are direct consumption benefits involved. The child is a source of pleasure in and of itself. Since we cannot observe directly the consumption value of which a child provides its family, it must be assumed that the values for preventing a birth which we have derived in this chapter relate to unwanted births. This topic is discussed further in Chapter VI. It is the economic consequences of a birth with which we are principally concerned in the present analysis. But even the analysis of the economic benefits has generated a controversy as to whether we should treat them differently according to whether they occur to the family or to the society outside the family.

Throughout the present chapter we have laid great stress on the important role that welfare criteria have in determining the value of preventing a birth. The question of the proper measure of welfare has been a central issue in the literature. Especially important in this regard is the critique of Enke made originally by Krueger and Sjastaad[21] and later renewed by Simon[22] and Demeny. All of these authors point out that most of the economic benefits from a reduction in family size are enjoyed by the family and only a relatively small residual portion is shared by the wider society. They feel that Enke erred in considering the benefits which accrue to the family as a result of birth prevention to be part of the social return to family planning. The benefits in question are, according to this viewpoint, internal to the family and not relevant to social decisions. The argument is basically that Enke was using the wrong welfare criterion.

The present chapter uses welfare criteria that are different than those suggested by either Enke or his critics. But in this sense at least our position is closer to that of Enke than to that of his detractors. The benefits as we suggest they should be measured include the return to both the immediate family and to the wider society. They do not include the psychological costs that were mentioned in a previous paragraph.

It seems clear from the plan documents that, except in the case of the very wealthy, planners have never divided the returns to planning into categories according to who reaps the benefits. There are many fields such as education, health and even agriculture where most of the benefits from planning accrue to individuals who should be willing to pay for all or most of the services which they enjoy. Nevertheless the privately enjoyed benefits which result from government investment are considered to be a part of the social return from planning. In any case the present chapter has treated both the returns to the family and the returns outside the family as legitimate social returns to the government investment. Our impression is that this approach is fully consistent with that adopted by Indian planners. In Chapter IV the results of our analysis will be applied to an analysis of the benefits and the costs of the Program as a whole.

NOTES

1. Good discussions of the concept of economic welfare and operational equivalents are to be found in Eckstein, "Theory of Public Expenditure Criteria," pp. 439–494, and in Harvey Leibenstein, "Why Do We Disagree on Investment Policies for Development?" in Readings in Economic Development, eds., Morgan, Betz, and Choudhry (Belmont, Calif.: Wadsworth, 1963), pp. 128–143.
2. Myrdal, Asian Drama, Chapter II.
3. See the introductory chapters of the Indian plans for a discussion of planning objectives; for example, Government of India, Planning Commission, Third Five Year Plan (New Delhi, 1961), Chapter I, pp. 1–19.
4. W. Galenson and Harvey Leibenstein, "Investment Criteria, Productivity and Economic Development," Quarterly Journal of Economics, 69 (Aug. 1955) pp. 343–70. Also, Stephen Enke, "Speculations on Population Growth and Economic Development," Quarterly Journal of Economics, 71 (Feb. 1953), pp. 19–35.

5. This part of Chapter II is based on work presented to a seminar at the Institute of Economic Growth, New Delhi, during December 1966. The computations have been reworked and extended with the computational facilities available in Berkeley and Ann Arbor.

6. Joseph Spengler, "Economics & Demography" in *The Study of Population*, edited by Philip Hauser and O. D. Duncan (Chicago: University of Chicago Press, 1959)), pp. 791–831. Joseph Spengler, "The Economist and the Population Question," *American Economic Review*, 56 (March 1966), pp. 1–24. Paul Demeny, *Demo-Graphic Aspects of Saving, Investment, Employment and Productivity*, background paper, United Nations World Population Conference, 1965. Paul Demeny, "Investment Allocation and Population Growth," *Demography*, 2 (1965), pp. 203–216 and "The Economics of Population Control," a paper prepared for the 1969 General Conference of the International Union for the Scientific Study of Population, Sept. 3–11, 1969, London, England. George C. Zaidan, "Population Growth and Economic Development," *Studies in Family Planning*, 42 (May, 1969), pp. 1–6. Warren Robinson and David Horlacker, "Evaluating the Economic Benefits of Fertility Reduction," *Studies in Family Planning*, 39 (March, 1969), pp. 4–8. Gorain Ohlin, *Population Control and Economic Development* (Paris: OEDC, 1967), pp. 53–64. Simon Kuznets, "Population and Economic Growth," *Proceedings of the American Philosophic Society*, 3 (June, 1967). Gavin Jones, "The Economic Effect of Declining Fertility in Less Developed Countries," An Occasional Paper of the Population Council, New York, 1969.

7. The plan projections are based upon the work of the Expert Committee on Population Projections for the Planning Commission. The survivorship assumptions used in the projection are those used by the committee in their favored projection.

8. India, Planning Commission, *Fourth Five Year Plan, 1969–74: Draft*, Delhi, n.d., p. 29. The actual projection of a national income that was used is that generated by the high-population estimate of Example III. It was used to make the resulting estimates as comparable as possible. In the strict sense Example I is not comparable with Examples II and III, since the projected path of national income is independent of population growth. In fact the projection could take on any value, and the results will vary accordingly. It does not seem unreasonable on the other hand to make comparisons which take the form of, "If conditions are accurately described by the assumptions of Example I, the value

of preventing a birth is X and if they are better described by Example II, the value of preventing a birth is Y."

9. Paul Demeny, "Investment Allocation and Population Growth," *Demography*, 2 (1965), pp. 203–232; Coale and Hoover, *Population Growth and Economic Development*.

10. This sensible hypothesis has been repeated often in the literature: Chap. XVI in Coale and Hoover, *Population Growth and Economic Development*; Demeny, "Investment Allocation"; T. J. Samuel, "Population Growth and Per Capita Income in Underdeveloped Economics," *Asian Economic Review*, 6 (Nov. 1963), p. 37; and P. R. Brahmananda's Introduction to V. R. M. Desai, *Social Aspects of Savings* (Bombay: Population Prakashan, 1967), p. xii; Nathaniel H. Leff, "Dependency Rates and Savings Rates," *The American Economic Review*, 59 (Dec. 1969), pp. 886–896. Empirical evidence concerning the validity of the hypothesis for India is much harder to find. Consequently, we are obliged to resort to pure theory in making the assertion. There have been budget studies made in the West that tend to confirm the hypothesis. See, for example, W. Eizenga, *Demographic Factors and Savings* (Amsterdam: North Holland, 1961). A contrary view of the relationship between saving (or investment) and population growth is postulated by Boserup, who suggests that countries or cultures faced with population pressure tend to invest and to adjust their technology to the size of the population. Personally, I do not find her evidence to be very convincing, except in the case of the movement from slash-and-burn cultivation to fixed cultivation. Ester Boserup, *The Conditions of Agricultural Growth* (Chicago: Aldine Publishing Company, 1965). See also Albert O. Hirschman, *The Strategy of Economic Development* (New Haven: Yale University Press, 1958), and Colin Clark, *Population Growth and Land Use* (New York: St. Martin's Press, 1967).

11. The rather arbitrary marginal decimals were necessitated by internal computing considerations but would appear to be of the proper order of magnitude.

12. Robert M. Solow, "Technical Change and the Aggregate Production Function," *Review of Economics and Statistics,* 39 (August, 1957), pp. 312–320.

13. E. T. Denison, *Why Growth Rates Differ,* (Washington, D.C.: Brookings Institution, 1967); and Everett E. Hagen and Oli Hawryhyshyn, "Analysis of World Income and Growth," *Economic Development and Cultural Change,* 18, No. 1, part II (Oct., 1969), special supplement.

14. T. W. Schultz, "Reflections on Investment in Man," *Journal of Political Economy*, 70 (Oct., 1962), pp. 1–8; Gary Becker, "Investment in Human Capital: A Theoretical Analysis," *Journal of Political Economy*, 70 (Oct., 1962), pp. 9–49; A good selection and further references are contained in Mark Blaug, editor, *Economics of Education 1* (Baltimore: Penguin Books Inc., 1968). See also Myrdal, *Asian Drama*, pp. 1533–1553.

15. Gavin Jones and P. Gingrich, "The Effects of Differing Trends in Fertility and of Educational Advance on the Growth, Quality, and Turnover of the Labor Force," *Demography*, 5, No. 1 (1968) pp. 226–248.

16. Increased population growth has two effects on the demand for food. First, more population means more demand just to maintain per capita consumption. Second, the lower incomes associated with the higher population situation tend to reduce demand. In the Indian context, despite the fact that the income elasticity of demand for food grains is high, the former effect probably outweighs the latter.

17. There have been many efforts in India to measure unemployment. Most have used Western concepts of full employment. In fact, the Western approach may be inappropriate to Indian conditions where employment at low or decreasing levels of productivity may limit the meaningfulness of conventional unemployment statistics. See Myrdal, *Asian Drama*, Chapters 21–26 and Appendix 6.

18. Myrdal, *ibid.*, has a useful discussion of the effects of population growth on landholdings. See pp. 1047–1052.

19. My feeling is that planners have often thought of the two objectives as synonymous. Thus, a great deal of emphasis on the "standard of living" does not preclude the possibility that planners might use national income as the nominal objective function.

20. Coale and Hoover, *Population Growth and Economic Development*; Enke, "The Gains to India from Population Control." See also, Enke, "The Economics of Government Payments," and the comment by Demeny (641–644) and the rejoinder by Enke (645–648) in the July 1961 issue of the same journal.

21. Anne O. Krueger and L. A. Sjastaad, "Some Limitations of Enke's Economics of Population," *Economic Development and Cultural Change*, 10 (July 1962), pp. 423–426.

22. Julian L. Simon, "The Value of Avoided Births to Underdeveloped Countries," *Population Stulies*, 23, No. 1 (March 1969), pp. 61–68.

CHAPTER THREE

Births Prevented In India Through the Use of the Intra-uterine Contraceptive Device and Sterilization

THE AIM of these first chapters is to assess the economic impact of past investments in family planning. In Chapter II we discussed the value of preventing a birth in contemporary India. In the present chapter we will go one step further by analyzing the number of births prevented by each insertion of an intra-uterine contraceptive device (IUD) or by each sterilization operation. These two methods are chosen, not because they are the only means of birth prevention encouraged by the Program, but because they are the only ones for which the number of users is regularly recorded in the official, published statistics.

The following analysis of births prevented by the IUD and sterilization is intended to serve as a bridge between the service statistics (the normal administrative record of the number of users) and the economic analysis of the previous chapter.[1] The number of births prevented is the difference between the number of births that would take place in the absence of the Program and the number that do take place with the Program in existence. The computational and analytic problems involved make this measure of program output very difficult. There are two possible approaches to estimating number of births prevented. The "direct" approach takes observed changes in fertility as its point of departure. The obvious difficulty is that fertility can change for many reasons among which the services and information provided by the Program is only one. In order to get an exact measure of demographic impact, we would have to have a method for separating Program-caused fluctuations in fertility from other fluctuations. Although we can make inferences about the extent of program influence, we cannot at this stage place very much faith in the exactitude of the estimates involved. Moreover, in the case of India, information about fertility is so inadequate as to rule out any effort to measure Program impact through the use of fertility data.

The "indirect" approach combines information about the people who use family planning services with other information to estimate the number of births prevented by the average couple using a contraceptive method. We employ the indirect approach in this chapter. It should be noted that this method of assessing program impact presents just as many analytic problems as does the direct approach, but the problem of obtaining the requisite data is somewhat more tractable. Ideally, if we had full information and an acceptable method for separating Program-induced change from others, the direct and the indirect measures of Program impact would give us the same results. In the present instance we do not have any choice but to use the second method.

There are some methodological remarks which should preface the relatively technical analysis that follows. We are attempting to discover the net impact of sterilization and the IUD on Indian fertility performance. We do so by examining the characteristics of adoptors and making some assumptions about the fertility they would have experienced if they had not used the government-sponsored forms of birth prevention. It should be clear that we cannot examine the same women, both using the IUD and *not* using it simultaneously. Therefore, the entire analysis hinges upon a set of essentially unverifiable assumptions.

Our most important assumption is that the fertility of adoptors can be represented by the average fertility of women in the wife's age class as corrected for the probability of secondary sterility. Adopting couples are special in a number of respects. They are of relatively high parity for their age class, and just the fact that they have decided to adopt the IUD or sterilization means that they are somewhat more motivated than couples in similar circumstances who do not use contraception. On the other hand, the women may be even more fecund than the average women in the age class, and part of their differential tendency to accept sterilization or the IUD may result from their accessibility to clinics and advice. Thus, there are a great many uncertainties involved in trying to strike an accurate balance, but certainly our assumption about alternative fertility patterns is a strong one. Means of modifying the assumption are discussed in the last section of the chapter and there is further discussion of the subject in Chapter V.

On a more practical level there are also important problems in dealing with data. In India there has been no attempt to construct a body of data which is fully representative of the couples using contraception in India. Thus, we are obliged to use data that refers to particular regions or sub-groups that have been the subject of surveys or other kinds of study. Some of the difficulties involved in the data will be made clear as the discussion proceeds.

The computations involved in estimating the number of births prevented are demanding, and it is important to justify the work involved. There are a number of alternative techniques for estimating the demographic impact of family planning acceptors. The simplest index of demographic impact would be the number of family planning acceptors or the percentage of the population which is accepting family planning. This very simple use of service statistics to measure output ignores both the important differences in the demographic impact of alternative contraceptive techniques which can be employed by users and the characteristics of individual users. For example, a vasectomy is likely to have more impact than a condom or an IUD.

A more sophisticated measure which has been much used recently is the "couple years of protection" or "CYP." This measure, originally introduced by Wishik,[2] has the advantage of being easily applied to the kind of service statistics that are produced by almost all family planning programs. Basically the procedure for estimating CYP's consists of estimating the number of years of protection provided by each family planning adoption. Thus, for the IUD, the procedure consists of determining the average amount of time that a woman is protected against the risk of pregnancy through the use of the IUD. Using this information and similar estimates for other program-sponsored methods of preventing births, it is possible to derive an estimate of the demographic impact of the program. The estimate has the important advantage of being a single number. In other words, the CYP is basically a mechanism for translating the very different demographic impact of sterilization, the IUD, and the other forms of contraception into a single homogeneous unit of measure.

For our purposes the CYP is a step in the right direction, but since it does not give us an estimate of the number of births prevented by the different methods, we cannot use it as a measure of program output. The economic value of a CYP depends on the number of births prevented. The number of births prevented will in turn depend on the age distribution of acceptors, their alternative patterns of fertility and the stage in the birth cycle when the method is introduced. This information is not contained in the CYP. Some refinements can, of course, be built into the CYP measure; but, if they are, many of the advantages of the measure are lost. In any case, with the same work that would be required to make extensive modifications in the CYP index, we can proceed directly to estimate the numbers of births prevented.

BIRTHS PREVENTED THROUGH THE USE OF IUD

Perhaps the most outstanding characteristic of the IUD is its semi-permanance. It is neither permanent in its effect upon fecundity as is sterilization, nor must it be applied with each act of coitus as must conventional contraceptives. To be effective in preventing births the IUD must be used by women who could possibly become pregnant if they were not protected by the device. There are then three problems in estimating the number of births prevented through the use of the IUD. First, we must know how long the device would continue in use. Second, we must differentiate between the useful retention of the device and the superfluous protection that takes place when the couple using the device is not fecund. Finally, we must estimate the alternative fertility in the absence of the device.

The method used to estimate the number of births "prevented" or "averted" is that developed by Robert G. Potter.[3] Potter's method takes into account the length of use of the IUD, the age distribution of the users, the possibility of death or secondary sterility interrupting a marriage during the period when the IUD is being employed, the overlap between amenorrhea and the use of the IUD, accidental pregnancies during the period when the IUD is being employed, and alternative assumptions concerning the fertility that would have been experienced by the adopters had they never used the IUD. The analysis at each stage is complicated and only a minimum amount of explanation is given here.[4] It should be noted that the discussion in the first part of the chapter deals with the first segment of IUD use only, i.e., with the period between the initial insertion and the first termination.

Women who are not permanently sterile are in one of three states characterizing the birth cycle. At any given time, a certain proportion of the married female population is pregnant, another proportion is in a condition of postpartum amenorrhea, and a third group is fecund. The essential function of the IUD, or of any other contraceptive technique, is the prolongation of the fecundable condition. This prolongation reduces the total number of pregnancies associated with the child-bearing period of a woman's life.[5] Potter's technique for estimating the number of births prevented by contraceptive use consists of finding the ratio of months of prolongation of the fecund state to months that the birth cycle would otherwise have involved. Two equations are involved in the estimation procedure.

(1) $I = F(R - A - PW)$ where all durations are in months, and

$I =$ average duration that childbearing is interrupted, i.e. the mean prolongation of the stay in the fecundable state

$F =$ the proportion of couples fecund at the time the IUD is inserted

$R =$ mean time the IUD is retained in the presence of mortality and sterility among couples fecund at the time of insertion

A = allowance for amenorrhea

P = proportion accidentally pregnant while using the IUD

W = penalty per accidental pregnancy

(2) $B = I/D$ where

B = births prevented per first segment of IUD

D = average duration per birth that might have been required had the IUD not been adopted

Discussion of the estimation procedure will be conducted according to the order suggested by these formulas.

Analysis is carried out by age class. It is assumed that the average age in each class is the midpoint of the class. Women younger than 20 years have been lumped with those 20 to 24, and the age 22.5 is assumed to be the mean for the group. Similarly, all women older than 40 have been lumped together, and it is assumed that their average age is 42.5. It is unlikely that this assumption distorts the age distribution very much.[6]

The Proportion of Women Fecund at the Time the IUD was Inserted[7]

F, the proportion of women fecund at the time the IUD was inserted, has been estimated with the use of data presented by S. N. Agarwala.[8] His data show the percentages of women in each five-year age group that is estimated to be secondarily sterile. By comparing the percentages of women sterile in two successive five year age groups it is possible to estimate the rate at which a particular cohort is likely to become sterile as they get older. We assume that each IUD user was fecund at the time her last pregnancy was terminated. The incidence of sterility at insertion is estimated by assuming that the rate of incidence of sterility established for the age group had applied to the group for the average length of time between the last pregnancy termination and the insertion.

THE MEAN TIME THAT THE IUD IS RETAINED—R

The greatest difficulty in estimating the effectiveness of the IUD is that unlike sterilization, it does not necessarily afford permanent protection. Potter suggests the term "EUROD" as a shorthand for "end of useful retention of the device." EUROD can be caused by mortality, by sterility, or by the combination of pregnancy, expulsion, and removal (PER). The components of EUROD are presented in Table III-1, and the proportion of EUROD attributable to each of these three causes is shown in Table III-2. PER is the largest

TABLE III-1
R: SPAN OF USEFUL RETENTION OF THE IUD—
ALLOWING FOR MORTALITY AND STERILITY
(IN COMPARISON WITH AN UNCORRECTED ESTIMATE)—
By AGE CLASS OF WIFE

Age Class	Monthly Rates of Attrition				Prop. Losing Device at Once[d]	Mean Span of Retention		$U - R$
	PER[a] p	Mort.[b] m	Ster.[c] s	Sum u		Corrected $R = \frac{(1-x)}{u}$	Uncorrected $U = \frac{(1-x)}{p}$	
−24	.0411	.00074	.00124	.04308	.0928	21.06	22.07	1.01
25–29	.0351	.00089	.00215	.03814	.0858	23.97	26.05	2.08
30–34	.0302	.00089	.00536	.03645	.0562	25.89	31.25	5.36
35–39	.0215	.00094	.01542	.03786	.0914	24.00	42.26	18.26
40+	.0241	.00094	.00827	.03331	.0572	28.30	39.12	10.82

[a] Estimates of PER derived as follows: $u(18)/u(6) = e^{-12p}$ and solving for p, where $u(18)$ and $u(6)$ represent the proportion of women retaining the IUD after 18 months and 6 months respectively. For the youngest cohort,

TABLE III-2

Proportions of Women Ending Useful Retention of the IUD Because of Mortality, Secondary Sterility, and PER (Pregnancy, Expulsion, or Removal), by Age Class of Wife[a]

Age Class	PER	Mort.	Secondary Sterility	Total
–24	.96	.02	.03	1.00
25–29	.93	.02	.05	1.00
30–34	.84	.02	.14	1.00
35–39	.61	.02	.37	1.00
40+	.74	.03	.23	1.00

[a] The proportions of women ending useful retention of the IUD due to PER, mortality, and secondary sterility were derived as follows:

$$\text{Proportion PER} = (1-x)s/u,$$
$$\text{Proportion } m = x + (1-x)p/u$$
$$\text{Proportion } s = (1-x)m/u$$

where x, p, m, s, and u, are those values calculated for Table III-1. See Potter, "A Technical Appendix on Procedures Used in Manuscript, 'Estimating Births Averted in a Family Planning Program,'" (Mimeograph) June 1, 1967, p. 13.

because of the small number of cases, the estimate of PER is based on the experience between the sixth and the twelfth month. Retention rates were derived from life table analysis of survey data. See George B. Simmons, "The Indian Investment in Family Planning," Ph.D. Dissertation, University of California at Berkeley, 1967, Table XIII-5, p. 218.

[b] Estimates of mortality were derived as follows: $p_f p_m = d^{-12m}$, solving for m, where p_f and p_m represent the probabilities of surviving for a year for females and males respectively. Source of mortality rates: National Sample Survey, No. 76, *Fertility and Mortality Rates in India* (Delhi, 1963), p. 15. Mortality by sex, all India rural.

[c] Estimates of secondary sterility were derived by setting conditional probabilities of becoming sterile in the next 5 years, if fecund at the midpoint of the 5-year age interval is equal to $1-e^{-60s}$ and solving for s. $S(x+2.5, x+7.5) = 1-e^{-60s}$. Source of sterility estimates: S. N. Agarwala, *Some Problems of India's Population* (Bombay: K. K. Vora, 1966), p. 119.

[d] The proportion x of women who lose the IUD immediately was derived by solving for x in the equation $(1-x)e^{-18p} = u(18)$, where $u(18)$ is the retention rate after 18 months and p is the estimate derived for PER above.

contributing cause of EUROD in all age classes, but the effects of mortality and sterility are important in the older age groups. Mortality and the onset of secondary sterility would, of course, be expected to be more important among the older age groups. Their importance is increased here because the longer mean length of use of the device among the older age groups means that women in these categories are exposed for a longer period to the risk of mortality or secondary sterility.

A small proportion of the women who use the IUD lose it in the first month and, taking this minority into account, the proportion retaining the IUD at any time can be described by the formula,

Proportion retaining at time $T = (1-x)e^{-uT}$

where

x = proportion expelling the device immediately

u = the probability of terminating useful life of the device in any given month

T = number of months elapsed since insertion

e = the natural log base

The probability of ending useful life of the IUD is given by the expression

$$u = s + m + p$$

where

s = monthly probability of becoming sterile after having device inserted

m = monthly probability of the couple's marital life being broken by mortality

p = the probability of pregnancy, expulsion or removal (abbreviated as PER following Potter)

Data concerning retention have been taken from the results of a survey conducted in Haryana State in Northern India.[9] Mortality and sterility data come from the National Sample Survey and S. N. Agarwala, respectively.[10]

Given the formula for retention, the mean length of retention, R, is given by dividing the expression $(1-x)$ by u, the monthly rate at which useful retention of the IUD is terminated. Some stages in the computation of R are given in Table III-1. Also presented in that table is an estimate of U, a measure of the mean length of retention of the IUD which does not take sterility or mortality into account. It is clear that the consideration of mortality and sterility affects the computations sizably. Especially for the older age groups, the differences between R and U are considerable. This finding illustrates the value of undertaking the extra work involved in treating the competing risks of mortality and sterility.

Overlap Between IUD Retention and Amenorrhea—A

Those months during which a woman wears the IUD but is in a state of lactating amenorrhea do not contribute to any lengthening of the birth cycle. Therefore, the mean number of months of overlap, A, must be subtracted from R for each age group. A is computed from the distribution of respondents by intervals between last birth and insertion.[11] It is assumed, on the basis of research done in Punjab State in Northern India,[12] that the average length of lactating amenorrhea can be assumed to be nine months for the lowest age group and twelve months for all others. The overlap between retention and amenorrhea turns out to be about three months on the average for all age groups. Thus, A represents a significant correction to R.

The Effect of Accidental Pregnancies in Decreasing the Effectiveness of the IUD—PW

If the IUD were 100 percent effective, R would only need to be adjusted by A. In fact, however, some pregnancies do occur while the IUD is being employed; consequently, it is necessary to subtract from R the mean number of months required to offset these accidental pregnancies. The appropriate number is calculated by multiplying the proportion of pregnancies experienced during the use of the IUD, (P), by the "mean fecundable period that would be required per pregnancy among still fertile acceptors if they had not had a chance to elect IUD, (W)."[13] The resulting correction, PW, is quite small, but had the pregnancy rate been as high as that experienced in some countries, the correction would have been larger.[14]

The calculations made thus far permit the estimation of I, the mean extension in the length of the birth cycle. The final estimate is given in the last column of Table III-3. Due to its shorter-than-average span of useful retention, the youngest age group shows the shortest prolongation of the birth cycle. Among the older age groups, the longer retention is somewhat offset by a greater incidence of secondary sterility before insertion. The range for all age groups is between eighteen and twenty-two months.

THE FERTILITY OF IUD ACCEPTORS IN THE ABSENCE OF THE IUD

In order to estimate the effect of the Program, it is necessary to know D, the level of fertility that would have been experienced in the absence of the IUD. Potter's estimates of D for Taiwan are based on detailed information concerning the fertility of IUD users before the period of IUD use.[15] No such data are available for India. The potential fertility of the IUD adoptors is difficult to estimate. On the one hand, we know that the adoptors are of higher-than-average fecundity for their age groups, since the incidence of primary and secondary sterility is lower than it is in the general population. On the other hand, many of the IUD adoptors report having employed some form of contraception before adopting the IUD. Most of this contraceptive use was probably not very effective, but it is an important factor. A related complication is that many of the adoptors might have re-

TABLE III-3

I: THE INTERRUPTION OF CHILDBEARING BY THE IUD, BY AGE CLASS OF WIFE

Age Class	Proportion of Women Fecund at Insertion F	Span of Useful Retention R	Mean Overlap with Amenorrhea A	Proportion Accidentally Pregnant P	Penalty per Pregnancy W^a	Allowance for Pregnancy PW	Interruption of Childbearing $I=F(R\cdot A\cdot PW)$
-24	.994	21.06	2.51	.030	8.05	.24	18.20
25–29	.980	23.97	3.05	.016	9.29	.15	20.35
30–34	.956	25.89	3.10	.034	9.97	.34	21.46
35–39	.888	24.00	2.70	.004	12.39	.05	18.88
40+	.806	28.30	1.92	.007	17.13	.12	21.16

[a] W estimates vary according to the assumptions made about the fertility in the absence of the IUD.

sorted to sterilization in the absence of the IUD. It is known that the rate of sterilization dropped off in some regions after the introduction of the IUD.[16] Had the IUD never been introduced, it is reasonable to suppose that the trend in sterilizations would have continued to follow the pattern of increase in the early sixties. In our analysis, it is not necessary to adjust for sterilization explicitly, since we treat both the IUD and sterilization as part of the same program.

The estimate of D, the mean length of the birth interval in the absence of the IUD, is based upon the marital age specific fertility schedule given by the Registrar General[17] (see Table III-4). This schedule has been corrected for the incidence of primary and secondary sterility in the population of adoptors and converted into the form of birth intervals. The correction was made by multiplying each age specific fertility rate by the ratio of the proportion of adoptors fecund at the midpoint of the interval during which the IUD was employed to the proportion of women of the same age in the general population who were fecund.[18]

$$\begin{pmatrix} \text{Age Specific} \\ \text{Fertility in the} \\ \text{Absence of Device} \end{pmatrix} = \begin{pmatrix} \text{Age Specific} \\ \text{Marital Fertility in} \\ \text{General Population} \end{pmatrix}$$

$$\times \begin{pmatrix} \text{Proportion} \\ \text{Fecund Among} \\ \text{IUD Acceptors} \end{pmatrix} \bigg/ \begin{pmatrix} \text{Proportion Fecund} \\ \text{in General} \\ \text{Population} \end{pmatrix}$$

The proportion of fecund women decreases much more rapidly in the general population than it does in the population of IUD adoptors. This is a consequence of the fact that IUD adoptors are selected for their high fecundity. One could argue that the differential in the proportion fecund which is postulated here is an understatement. It may be argued on the basis of their relatively very high parity that, even within the category of fecund women, the degree of fecundity is higher among IUD acceptors than among the general population.

TABLE III-4

D: THE LENGTH OF THE BIRTH INTERVAL
IN THE ABSENCE OF THE IUD

Age Group	Age Specific Marital Fertility Rate[a]	Corrected for Age at Retention[b]	Proportion Acceptors Fecund[c]	Proportion All Women Fecund[c]	Corrected ASMFR of Acceptors[d]	D Birth Interval Months[e]
(1)	(2)	(3)	(4)	(5)	(6)	
−24	.295	.297	.977	.931	.311	38.57
25–29	.304	.298	.957	.865	.330	36.35
30–34	.275	.259	.907	.760	.309	38.84
35–39	.200	.183	.844	.551	.280	42.82
40+	.115	.096	.949	.219	.418	28.73

[a] *Source*: India, Registrar General, *Vital Statistics of India, 1961* (Delhi, 1964), p. LI.

[b] Correction Factor $= \dfrac{R/2}{60}X$ (first difference). For women aged 25–29,

Correction Factor $= \dfrac{11.985}{60}(-.029) = -.0058$. Therefore, the corrected ASMFR $= .304 + (-.0058) = .2982$.

[c] Data on sterility have been taken from Agarwala, *Some Problem's of India's Population*.

[d] Corrected ASMFR for acceptors = col. (3)/col. (4) × col. (2)

[e] $D = 12/\text{ASMFR}$ (in col. 5)

The number of births prevented by the IUD is measured by the ratio of I to D. Table III-5 gives an estimate of the number of births prevented per IUD insertion for each age group and for a weighted average of the entire population. The weights are taken from the Haryana IUD study. The corrected census estimate of alternative fertility gives an estimate of .54 births prevented for each IUD inserted.

DISCUSSION

Having gone through this lengthy procedure, how much certainty should be attached to the value of .54 births prevented per IUD inserted? There is no easy answer, but some

TABLE III-5

BIRTHS PREVENTED THROUGH USE OF THE IUD

Age Class	Proportion Women[a]	I	D	Births Prevented I / D
–24	.068	18.20	38.57	.47
25–29	.216	20.35	36.35	.56
30–34	.284	21.46	38.84	.55
35–39	.292	18.88	42.82	.44
40+	.140	21.16	28.73	.74
All Ages (Weighted Average)				.54

[a] Proportions are from the Haryana IUD study and based on a total of 1604. See Simmons, "The India Investment in Family Planning," p. 188.

discussion of the components of the estimate may make the matter clearer. The sterility data presented by Agarwala indicate that the level of secondary sterility is considerably higher among the Indian women he studied than among the French women whose fertility histories are the source of the data used by Potter. One of the characteristics of Indian fertility is that age specific marital fertility rates are lower in the age groups above thirty than in comparable age groups from European populations.[19] In any case, the secondary sterility assumptions are, if anything, on the high side. The same can be said of mortality as the rates used are calculated from data collected in 1958–59, and the general feeling is that mortality has been falling in the interim period.

The data concerning device loss and the age distribution of adoptors have been taken from the Haryana IUD Study.[20] In the absence of survey results from a large number of locations, it is difficult to assess the distortion introduced when the Haryana experience is generalized to all India. Most of the published studies of IUD use in India refer to the urban areas.[21] In those areas the rentention was higher than in Haryana, and the age distribution was slightly younger. Thus, the estimate of the number of births prevented through the use of the IUD is likely to be, if anything, an underestimate of the all-India figure. Unfortunately, given the gaps in our knowledge, it is difficult to attach too much certainty to this conclusion or to specify the magnitude of the distortion introduced by using data from one region of India.

The official statistics seem to treat reinsertions as if they were the equivalent of initial insertions. In Haryana reinsertions were about 2 percent of the total number recorded, but as the program matures the proportion of reinsertions reported in the statistics is likely to rise. If the average effect of a second or third segment of IUD use were the same as the first segment, no distortion would be introduced by treating all reported insertions as first insertions. The evidence, however, indicates that reinsertions tend to be retained for shorter periods than are the first insertions. Consequently their inclusion in the service statistics means that we are slightly overstating the effect of the IUD. The problem will become larger as the percentage of reinsertions among IUD users increases. As best one can tell, the effect of reinsertions on our conclusions is relatively small; we have chosen to ignore it in the rest of the discussion.

Many readers may ask themselves what shortcuts can be made in the estimation procedure described above. The most important informational inputs into the process are the level of alternative fertility, the retention rate, and the age distribution of the acceptors. A perfectly reasonable estimate of the number of births prevented through the use of the IUD could be made by using available data for those key variables and combining it with the data employed in the accompanying tables or that used by Potter in his calculations for Taiwan. Of course the estimates will become more reasonable the more closely the data employed in the calculations approximate the "true" situation. On the other hand, there is so much uncertainty involved in the whole process that it would be overly cautious to refuse to undertake an estimate of the birth-preventing impact of a program because all the data is not available. When exactly the right information is lacking, a passable substitute may be found in demographic data from populations that we believe to be similar to the one which is under study. For example, the fertility data may be lacking for exactly that population where the IUD was inserted, but we may be able to get adequate information from a different but similar population. It is especially likely that the detailed information underlying the calculations for PW and to a lesser extent A will be missing. In that case either the Taiwan or the Indian figures, whichever is more appropriate, could be used as a substitute.

The Distribution of Births Prevented by the IUD Over Time

Once having estimated the number of births that are prevented by the IUD, it is useful to estimate when they will be prevented. If we assume that the number of births prevented (B_K) in any year K after the insertion will be proportionate to the ratio of the number of months of useful retention during the year $K-1$ to the total number of months I by which the birth cycle is prolonged, then the number of births prevented in any given year is represented by the expression

$$B_K = I_{K-1}/D$$

We are assuming, then, that there is a one-year rather than a nine-month lag between a conception prevented and a birth prevented. Table III-6 presents the weighted average of the births prevented per insertion in each of the ten years following insertion. As one would expect, the birth-preventing effectiveness of the IUD is confined largely to the first few years after insertion.

TABLE III-6

BIRTHS PREVENTED BY YEAR AFTER INSERTION[a]

Year (K)	Births Prevented Per Insertion[b] (B_K)
0 (Year of Insertion)	0
1	.1539
2	.1388
3	.0890
4	.0571
5	.0367
6	.0236
7	.0152
8	.0098
9	.0063
10	.0040
11+	.0074
Total	.5418

[a] For methodology see Potter, "A Technical Appendix," pp. 19–21.
[b] These figures have been carried out to four decimal places, not to indicate false accuracy, but because rounding results in significant error.

BIRTHS PREVENTED THROUGH STERILIZATION

Many of the difficulties that loom so large in the estimation of the number of births prevented through the use of the IUD are less important or insignificant in analyzing the effects of sterilization. The effects of sterilization, however, make themselves felt over a much longer horizon and, consequently, the method of dealing with secondary sterility and mortality has a greater import than in the case of the IUD, where the loss of effectiveness of the device was largely due to PER (pregnancy, expulsion, or removal). There is little evidence of "contraceptive" failure in the case of sterilization.[22] The principal factors affecting the birth-preventing qualities of a sterilization program are the age distribution of the acceptors, their sterility characteristics relative to the general population of the age group, the fertility of the age group, and their mortality experience after the operation has been performed.

MORTALITY

Ignoring the possibility of remarriage, the probability of a marriage surviving any period intact has been calculated as the product of the probabilities of survival of the two individuals.[23] The mean number of surviving marriage units is assumed equal to the mean of the proportion surviving at the beginning of the interval and the proportion surviving at the end of the interval.

STERILITY

It is reasonable to assume that the persons resorting to sterilization are less frequently subfecund than the general population. Since virtually all sterilization cases have at least one child living at the time of the operation (most have three or more) primary sterility is nonexistent among them. Moreover, the general high parity of this group indicates that secondary sterility is less frequent than in the general population. In the absence of any data concerning the interval between last pregnancy termination and sterilization, we assume that the proportion, F, of couples fecund at the time of insertion of the IUD can represent the situation for sterilization as well. This assumption may still overstate fecundity somewhat, especially in areas where incentive payments have been widely employed.[24] On this assumption, and using Agarwala's data concerning secondary sterility, the proportion of women remaining fecund at different intervals after sterilization is given in Table III-9, and the proportion fecund at the midpoint of each five-year interval after insertion is given in Table III-10.

TABLE III-7

PROBABILITY OF MARRIAGE SURVIVING
BY AGE GROUP OF WIFE AT STERILIZATION[a]

Age Group	Age at Sterilization				
	To 24	25–29	30–34	35–39	40–44
TO 24	1.0000				
25–29	.9154	1.0000			
30–34	.8324	.9093	1.0000		
35–39	.7509	.8203	.9021	1.0000	
40–44	.6686	.7304	.8033	.8904	1.0000
45–49	.5819	.6357	.6991	.7750	.8703

[a] Mortality data have been taken from the U.N. Model Life Table 23 for males and Table 25 for females. These tables probably overstate mortality for India. United Nations, Department of Social Affairs, Population Studies, No. 22, *Age and Sex Patterns of Mortality: Model Life Tables for Under-Developed Countries* (New York, 1955), pp. 18–21.

TABLE III-8

MEAN PROPORTION SURVIVING DURING INTERVAL

Age at midpoint of interval after sterilization	Age at Sterilization				
	To 24	25–29	30–34	35–39	40–44
25	.9577				
30	.8739	.9547			
35	.7917	.8648	.9511		
40	.7098	.7754	.8527	.9452	
45	.6253	.6831	.7512	.8327	.9352

TABLE III-9

PROBABILITY OF REMAINING FECUND AT
THE END OF THE SPECIFIED FIVE YEAR INTERVAL

Age Group	Age at Sterilization				
	To 24	25–29	30–34	35–39	40–44[a]
To 24	.9938				
25–29	.9228	.9798			
30–34	.8113	.8614	.9559		
35–39	.5882	.6245	.6930	.8883	
40–44	.2332	.2476	.2748	.3523	.8058
45–49	.1420	.1507	.1673	.2144	.2500

[a] In the age group 40–44 we have assumed that the rate at which women become sterile is somewhat higher than would be indicated by Agarwala's data. If we had used Agarwala's numbers the proportion of users assumed fecund at the end of the 49th year would have been slightly over fifty percent. While it seems likely that a higher proportion of users than general population may be fecund in that age group, it is unlikely that figures would be that large.

TABLE III-10

PROPORTION FECUND AT MIDPOINT OF
FIVE YEAR INTERVAL AFTER STERILIZATION

Age at Midpoint of Interval	Age at Sterilization				
	To 24	25–29	30–34	35–39	40–44
25	.9583				
30	.8670	.9206			
35	.6997	.7429	.8245		
40	.4107	.4361	.4839	.6203	
45	.1876	.1992	.2211	.2833	.5279

TABLE III-11

OTHER DATA

Age at Midpoint of Interval After Sterilization	Proportion Fecund in General Population[a]	Age-Specific Marital Fertility[b]
25	.895	.301
30	.805	.290
35	.640	.238
40	.355	.153
45	.135	.075

[a] Computed from Agarwala's data on secondary sterility. Five percent primary sterility has been added to the secondary sterility rate. S. N. Agarwala, *Some Problems of India's Population.*

[b] From *Vital Statistics of India,* 1961, p. LI. The data were collected through a special survey and seem reasonably accurate; if it errs, it is on the low side. The age groups were computed from the original data by graphing. The data refer to the rural Punjab.

FERTILITY PERFORMANCE IN THE ABSENCE OF STERILIZATION

Given the above data, the ratio of births to original acceptors is given by the expression,

$$\begin{array}{c}\text{Births Prevented} \\ \text{Per Sterilization}\end{array} = \begin{array}{c}\text{Proportion} \\ \text{Surviving}\end{array} \times \begin{array}{c}\text{Relative Fecundity} \\ \text{of Persons Sterilized}\end{array} \times \begin{array}{c}\text{Age Specific} \\ \text{Marital Fertility}\end{array} \times 5$$

where the relative fecundity of persons sterilized in each age group is given by the ratio of the proportion fecund among sterilized couples to the proportion fecund in the general population. The total number of births prevented is then given by the sum of the births prevented in each cohort as it moves through each of the remaining five year intervals of the fertile period. Table III-12 shows the results of this computation. When the weighted average is taken, an estimate of the mean number of births prevented per sterilization is obtained. The figures are generally quite high.

TABLE III-12

BIRTHS PREVENTED PER STERILIZATION
WITH CORRECTION FOR THE RELATIVE
FECUNDITY OF THE PERSONS STERILIZED

Age at the Midpoint of Each Five-Year Interval After Sterilization	Age at Sterilization				
	To 24	25–29	30–34	35–39	40–44
25	1.5433				
30	1.3648	1.5830			
35	1.0300	1.1947	1.4580		
40	.6282	.7286	.8892	1.2634	
45	.3259	.3780	.4612	.6554	1.3713
Total	4.8921	3.8843	2.8084	1.9188	1.3713
Proportion in Age group[a]	.017	.129	.304	.285	.265
Births Averted Weighted Avg.	.0832	.5011	.8538	.5469	.3634

Weighted Average = 2.35

[a] Proportions taken from Thomas Poffenberger, "Age of Wives and Number of Living Children of a Sample of Men Who Had the Vasectomy in Meerut District, U.P.," *Journal of Family Welfare*, 13 (June 1967), pp. 48–51. These wives of vasectomy cases are slightly older than their counterparts in other regions of India.

Because sterilization is a permanent method, younger couples are less likely to use it than the IUD. Thus, the *age distribution* of users of the two techniques will vary considerably. When the actual age distribution of the wives of one sample of vasectomy cases in used,[25] the weighted average of the different ages at sterilization indicates that the mean number of *births prevented* by a sterilization is on the order of 2.35. Thus, each sterilization prevents slightly more than four times as many births as does the first segment of IUD usage. When the exercise of estimating the number of births prevented by a sterilization is repeated, assuming that the age-specific marital fertility rate of the entire population of women in the age group reasonably represents the likely fertility performance of those women who have been sterilized, the weighted average of the number of births prevented is 2.1, still greatly in excess of the number prevented through IUD insertions. The actual number prevented is probably closer to the higher figure.

THE DISTRIBUTION OF BIRTHS PREVENTED BY STERILIZATION OVER TIME

The distribution of births prevented by sterilization over the years following the operation has been accomplished by graphing, for each age group, the data of Table III-12, which refers to five year intervals, and interpolating from the graphs the figures for individual years. See Table III-13. It will be noted that most of the effect is felt within the first ten years. This result derives, in part, from the age distribution of the population of persons who have been sterilized; over 50 percent of the total have less than ten years left in the fecund age group. It has been assumed that no births will occur more than five years after the sterilization for the oldest age group. This assumption implies that fertility ceases at age 47.5.

TABLE III-13

BIRTHS PREVENTED BY YEAR AFTER STERILIZATION

Year	Births Prevented per Sterilization	Year	Births Prevented per Sterilization
0	.0	13	.0465
1	.3539	14	.0379
2	.3177	15	.0303
3	.2797	16	.0238
4	.2410	17	.0163
5	.2048	18	.0086
6	.1693	19	.0064
7	.1398	20	.0043
8	.1247	21	.0025
9	.1095	22	.0013
10	.0911	23	.0008
11	.0762	24	.0006
12	.0608	25	.0003
Total	2.3481	=	2.35 births prevented

THE NUMBER OF BIRTHS PREVENTED BY STERLIZATION OR THE IUD WHEN THE ASSUMPTIONS ABOUT ALTERNATIVE FERTILITY ARE CHANGED

In estimating the number of births prevented through the use of sterilization or the IUD, we have assumed that, in the absence of the device women would have experienced fertility equivalent to that of the average woman of similar fecundity in the same age class. It is possible that this assumption should be modified. If, in the absence of the government Family Planning Program, couples were practicing abstinence or using commercially available condoms, their fertility might be considerably lower than postulated. If we knew exactly what the alternatives to the IUD and sterilization were, and how effectively and by what percentage of adoptors they would be used, we could make some calculation of the net effectiveness of the IUD and sterilization. Our information on these issues is very fragmentary, however, and we will resort to a simpler approach to illustrate the effect on the impact of these birth control techniques.

Suppose that, in the absence of the IUD or sterilization, a certain percentage of women adoptors would have used some other means of limiting fertility and, further, that the technique of fertility limitation was exactly as effective as the clinical device (IUD or sterilization) which it replaced. Then, the average birth-preventing impact of IUD or sterilization would be reduced by the percentage of women who would have used another method of equal effectiveness. If 50 percent of the IUD adoptors, in the absence of the IUD, would have used equivalently effective methods, then the number of births prevented through the use of the IUD would have been reduced by 50 percent. In the case of the IUD, then, we are assuming that 50 percent of the acceptors who had alternatives would have experienced the same fertility using the alternative that they did with the IUD. That is, the number and timing of accidental pregnancies and the termination rate would be equivalent in the two cases. In the case of sterilization, the assumption is the equivalent of asserting that the alternative fertility in the absence of sterilization would have been zero for that proportion of adoptors who had alternatives.[26]

This result is very useful because it gives us a means of assessing the impact of the IUD and sterilization without assuming that all of the births prevented are associated with the existence of the Program. The simplicity of the adjustment required is the result of the strong assumption that the alternative method would have had exactly the same impact as the technique with which it was replaced. This assumption is, of course, unlikely to correspond with the actual situation. There is likely to be proportionately more awareness of alternatives in some age groups than in others.

The effectiveness of alternative means of birth prevention would almost certainly differ from that of the IUD or sterilization. The use of the condom, for example, is likely to be less effective than the use of sterilization, and the use of total abstinence is likely to be more effective than the use of the IUD. Despite its drawbacks, however, we will use the assumption in later chapters to illustrate the consequences for program effectiveness of assuming that women would have had alternative means of preventing births even if the government had not decided to invest in the Family Planning Program.

APPENDIX TO CHAPTER III

The following tables are intended to document the computations underlying the calculations involved in estimating the number of births prevented by the IUD.

TABLE III-14

ESTIMATING F, THE PROPORTION OF COUPLES FECUND AT TIME OF INSERTION, BY AGE OF WIFE[a]

Age Class	Proportion Sterile at Start of Interval[b]	First Difference	Conditional Probability of Sterily[c]	Mean Interval to Insertion[d] (months)	Proportion Expected to be Sterile at Insertion[e] $((4)/60)\times(3)$	Proportion F Fecund at Insertion[f] $F=1-(5)$
	(1)	(2)	(3)	(4)	(5)	(6)
–24	.020	—	.036	10.5	.006	.994
25–29	.055	.035	.095	12.7	.020	.980
30–34	.145	.090	.193	13.7	.044	.956
35–39	.310	.165	.413	16.2	.112	.888
40–44	.595	.285	.543	21.4	.194	.806
45–49	.815	.220	—	—	—	—

[a] See Potter, "A Technical Appendix on," pp. 7–8.
[b] S. N. Agarwala, *Some Problems of India's Population.*

Data needed for Calculation of F:

1. Proportion of the general population secondarily sterile in each age group.

2. Average interval in each age group between last pregnancy termination and the insertion of the IUD.

TABLE III-15

CALCULATION OF A, OVERLAP BETWEEN IUD RETENTION AND AMENORRHEA FOR WOMEN AGED 25–29 YEARS

Interval from Last Birth to Insertion of IUD (months) i	Midpoint	Proportion Women, Interval from Last Birth to Insertion[a] w_i	Overlap with Amenorrhea for Each Interval From Birth to Insertion[b] a_i	$w_i a_i$	Avg. Overlap Between IUD and Amenorrhea[c] A
0.0–2.9	1.5	.196	8.65	1.70	
3.0–5.9	4.5	.162	6.52	1.06	
6.0–8.9	7.5	.084	4.14	.35	
9.0–11.9	10.5	.159	1.46	.23	
12+	—	.399	—	—	
Total		1.000		3.34	3.05

[a] George B. Simmons, "The Indian Investment in Family Planning," Ph.D. Dissertation, University of California at Berkeley, 1967, Part II, p. 192.

[b] $a_i = (1/u) (1 - e^{-uT})$ For example, a_1 for age group 25–29 would be calculated as follows: $a_1 = (1/.03814) (1 - e^{-(.03814)(10.5)}) = 8.65$.

[c] $A = (1-x) \sum_{i=1}^{4} w_i a_i$. For women aged 25–29, $A = (.9142) (3.33) = 3.05$. See Potter, "A Technical Appendix," pp. 14–15.

---

[e] The conditional probability of sterility for the first age group, [row (1) of column (3)] is calculated by dividing the change in the proportion sterile between the first two age groups [row (2) of column (2)] by the proportion fecund in the first age group [1 − row (1) of column (1)].

[d] George B. Simmons, *The Indian Investment in Family Planning*.

[•] Col. (5) = (Col. (4)/60) × Col. (3). For example, for women aged 25–29, the proportion expected to be sterile at insertion would be computed as follows: 12.7/60(.095) = .0202.

[f] $F = 1 -$ Col. (5).

Data needed for Calculation of A:

1. Average period of amenorrhea following a live birth, by age of mother.

2. Proportion of women by age whose interval from last birth to first insertion of the IUD is 0–2.9 months, 3.0–5.9 months, 6.0–8.9 months, 9.0–11.9 months, and 12 months or more.

3. Overlap T of IUD retention with amenorrhea, varying according to the difference between length of amenorrhea for a given age group of women and the mean number of months from last birth to insertion. T is easily calculated by subtracting the midpoint (above) from the average length in months of amenorrhea. For example, $T_1 = 12.0 - 1.5 = 10.5$; $T_2 = 12.0 - 4.5 = 7.5$; etc.

TABLE III-16

CALCULATION OF P, PROPORTION OF WOMEN
ACCIDENTALLY PREGNANT WHILE USING THE IUD

Age	Proportion IUD loss Attributable to PER[a]	Proportion Women Fecund at Time of Insertion[b] F	Mean Span of IUD Retention[c]	Net Yearly Pregnancy Rates[d]	Net Monthly Pregnancy Rates[e] r	Proportion Women Accidentally Pregnant P
–24	.9583	.9938	21.06	.018	.00150	.0299
25–29	.9271	.9798	23.97	.009	.00075	.0163
30–34	.8382	.9559	25.89	.020	.00167	.0342
35–39	.6074	.8883	24.00	.004	.00033	.0043
40+	.7393	.8058	28.30	.005	.00042	.0070

[a] See Table III-2.
[b] See Table III-3.
[c] See Table III-3.
[d] The net pregnancy rates after 12 months are from the survey reported in George B. Simmons, *The Indian Investment in Family Planning*, Ph.D. Dissertation, University of California at Berkeley, 1969. For gross pregnancy rates, see page 218.
[e] The net monthly pregnancy rates were derived by solving for p in the following equation:

Net yearly pregnancy rates $= 1 - e^{-12p}$.

4. Monthly probability u of ending useful retention of the IUD, through PER, mortality, and secondary sterility. See Table III-1.

5. Proportion of women $(1-x)$ who lose the IUD at once. See Table III-1.

Data needed to Calculate P:

1. Proportion of women fecund at time of insertion of the IUD, by age.

2. Proportion of IUD loss attributed to PER (pregnancy, expulsion, and removal), by age.

3. Mean time in months that the IUD is retained, by age.

4. Net monthly pregnancy rates for women using the IUD, by age.

Data Needed for the Calculation of W, Penalty per Pregnancy:

1. Length of pregnancy in months.

2. Length in months of post-partum amenorrhea, by age.

3. Proportion of pregnancies lost to spontaneous abortion.

4. Proportion of pregnancies lost to stillbirths.

5. Number of months lost due to combined periods of pregnancy and amenorrhea associated with spontaneous fetal wastage.

6. Number of pregnancies per live birth.

7. Age-specific fertility rates, adjusted for the decline in fertility during the months of retention of the IUD. These rates are needed for the calculation of D', the total duration per birth required had the IUD not been adopted.

Data Needed for the Calculation of F, Proportion of Women Fecund at Insertion

1. Mean interval in months from last birth to first insertion of the IUD, by age.

2. Proportion of women sterile at the start of the five year age interval, needed to calculate the conditional probability of becoming sterile before age $x+5$ years if still fecund at age x years.

TABLE III-17

CALCULATION OF W, FECUNDABLE MONTHS PER PREGNANCY[a]

Class Age	Length of Pregnancy	Post-partum Amenorrhea[b]	Period of Pregnancy and Amenorrhea Associated with Fetal Wastage[c]	Non-Fecundable Months per Live Birth (1)+(2)+(3)	D', Duration Per Live Birth[d]	Fecundable Months per Live Birth (5)−(4)	Pregnancies Per Live Birth[e]	W, Fecundable Months Per Pregnancy [(5)−(4)]/(7)
	(1)	(2)	(3)	(4)	(5)	(6)	(7)	(8)
−24	9.0	9.4	.76	19.2	28.18	9.02	1.12	8.05
25–29	9.0	10.7	.76	20.5	30.87	10.41	1.12	9.29
30–34	9.0	12.3	1.05	22.4	34.21	11.86	1.19	9.97
35–39	9.0	12.9	1.05	23.0	37.70	14.75	1.19	12.39
40+	9.0	13.5	1.05	23.6	43.93	20.38	1.19	17.13

[a] See Potter, "A Technical Appendix," pp. 17–18, and Table A-3.

[b] Potter, et al., "A Case Study of Birth Interval Dynamics," *Population Studies* 19, July 1965, Table 1, p. 86.

[c] Estimates of this row were derived as follows: (1.0/.89)[.08(4) + .03(12)] = 0.76, and (1.0/.84) [.13(4) + .03(12)] = 1.05. These estimates assume that out of 100 pregnancies, 8 will end in spontaneous abortions (13 in the older age groups) and 3 will end in stillbirths. Four months and twelve months represent the lengths of gestation and amenorrhea associated with these pregnancy outcomes. Source of data for these estimates: *Ibid.*

Estimates of W depend on detailed assumptions about the fecundity of each age class including rates of spontaneous pregnancy wastage, length of gestation and amenorrhea. These assumptions are used to determine the number of pregnancies required to produce a live birth.

Table "X" shows the analysis leading to the final W estimates. After calculating D, the total duration per birth required in the absence of the IUD, as well as the values for (1) length of pregnancy, (2) post-partum amenorrhea, and (3) pregnancy and amenorrhea associated with spontaneous fetal wastage, one can derive the total fecundable period per birth as a residual. Division of this residual by the number of pregnancies per live birth yields the value of W in months.

NOTES

1. Readers who are faced with the responsibility of evaluating programs which stress methods such as oral contraceptive can take comfort in the fact that the demographic impact of the "pill" can be analyzed using an approach very similar to that described for the IUD. See Robert G. Potter, "Application of Life Table Techniques to Measurement of Contraceptive Effectiveness," *Demography*, 3, No. 2 (1966), pp. 297–304, and Christopher Tietze, "Intra-uterine Contraception: Recommended Procedures for Data Analysis," *Studies in Family Planning*, 18 (Supplement), (April 1967), pp. 1–6.

2. Samuel M. Wishik, "Indexes for Measurement of Amount of Contraceptive Practice," presented at meeting of Expert Group on Assessment of Acceptance and Use-Effectiveness of Family Planning Methods, United Nations Economic Commission for Asia and the Far East, Bangkok, Thailand, June 11–21, 1968. For other information on the use of the CYP concept and other measures of demographic impact see W. Parker Mauldin, "Births Averted by Family Planning Programs," *Turkish Demography: Proceedings of a Conference*, edited by Frederic C. Shorter and Bozkurt Güvenc, (Turkey: Hucettepe University, Institute of Population Studies), 1969, pp. 281–297, reprinted in condensed form in *Studies in Family Planning*, 33 (Aug. 1968), pp. 1–7. See also Lee R. Bean and William Seltzer, "Couple Years of Protection and Births Prevented: A Methodological Examination," *Demography*, 5, No. 2 (1968), pp. 947–959.

3. Robert G. Potter, "Estimating Births Averted in a Family Planning Program," in *Fertility and Family Planning: A World View*, edited by Samuel J. Behrman, Leslie Corsa, and Ronald Freedman (Ann Arbor: The University of Michigan Press, 1969), pp. 413–434. Also, "A Technical Appendix on Procedures Used in Manuscript, 'Estimating Births Averted in a Family Planning Program'," prepared for Major Ceremony V, University of Michigan Sesquicentennial celebration by Robert G. Potter (mimeographed, June 1, 1967).

4. An attempt has been made to present the tables in such a manner that the calculation can be reconstructed without excessive difficulty. The tables appearing in the text include material that seems relevant to a general understanding of the results obtained. Supplementary tables that might be necessary for a reconstruction of the results are contained in an appendix to the chapter.

5. On the assumption that the woman is not just delaying a pregnancy as might be the case in a population with widespread birth control.

6. Users in the age group 20–24 are probably older on the average than 22.5, the midpoint in the interval; consequently the addition of the few younger women to the age group probably serves as a corrective, bringing the average age of users in the age class closer to 22.5. The same is true in reverse for the older age groups.

7. The detailed computations underlying the calculation of F are presented in Table III-14 in the appendix to this chapter.

8. S. N. Agarwala, *Some Problems of India's Population* (Bombay: K. K. Vora, 1966), p. 119.

9. George B. Simmons, "The Indian Investment in Family Planning," Ph.D. Dissertation, University of California, Berkeley, 1967, Table XIII-5.

10. National Sample Survey, No. 76, *Fertility and Mortality Rates in India* (Delhi, 1963), p. 15. Agarwala, *Some Problems*.

11. See Chapter Appendix, Table III-15, for the details of computation.

12. Robert G. Potter, *et al.*, "A Case Study of Birth Interval Dynamics," *Population Studies*, 19 (July 1965), pp. 81–96.

13. Potter, "Estimating Births Averted," p. 419. See Chapter Appendix, Tables III-16 and III-17, for the computations.

14. See the discussion of the termination of the use of IUD through accidental pregnancy in Simmons, "The Indian Investment in Family Planning," Chapter XIII. The fact that the pregnancy rate is lower in India than in Taiwan seems largely a function of the size of the IUD used in the program.

15. Potter, "Estimating Births Averted," pp. 426–429. See also "Comparative Fertility of the IUD Acceptors and of all Married Women

of Childbearing Age in Taiwan," Ronald Freedman and Anrudh K. Jain, Taiwan Population Studies, Working Paper No. 3, Population Studies Center, University of Michigan, (mimeograph). And *Family Planning in Taiwan: An Experiment in Social Change*, Ronald Freedman and John Y. Takeshita (Princeton, N.J.: Princeton University Press, 1969), pp. 280–291.

16. Simmons, "Indian Investment in Family Planning," Table X-1.

17. India, Registrar General, *Vital Statistics of India, 1961* (Delhi, 1965), p. iv.

18. Data on sterility have been taken from Agarwala, *Some Problems*.

19. The reasons for this pattern are unknown. It is quite possible that abstinence, or some other form of fertility control, may play an important role, and if that is the case, the assumption of no other method being used may really imply that, in the absence of the IUD, the same use of abstinence would continue.

20. Simmons, "The Indian Investment in Family Planning," Part II.

21. See, for example, S. N. Agarwala, "A Follow-up Study of Intra-Uterine Contraceptive Device: An Indian Experience" (mimeographed, New Delhi, 1967); or H. Khrishna Rao, "A Study of IUD Cases in Bangalore," *Family Planning News*, 3 (March and April, 1968). Using the age distributions found by either Agarwala or Rao in the populations which they studied reduces the number of births prevented from .54 to .53. Using Agarwala's retention data and the Haryana age distribution raises the estimate of the number of births prevented to .79. Agarwala studied an experimental group of acceptors in the national capital, and it is exceedingly unlikely that their experience can be projected to the rest of India.

22. There have been reports of conceptions during the three months following a vasectomy, but such cases are infrequent.

23. Remarriage is perhaps less likely in India than in many other cultures, but a refinement of the calculation procedure would be to adjust for it. Mortality data have been taken from the UN Model Life Table 23 for males and Table 25 for females. These tables probably overstate mortality for India. United Nations, Department of Social Affairs, Population Studies, No. 22, *Age and Sex Patterns of Mortality: Model Life Tables for Under-Developed Countries* (New York, 1955), pp. 18–21.

24. During recent years there has been an increasing tendency to give incentive payments both to the sterilization case and to the person who recruits the case. The use of incentives is likely to encourage sterilizations for couples where there is little risk of pregnancy. There is some evidence that a significant proportion (say one-

third) of the cases recruited in some areas for Madras are older than fifty or unmarried or otherwise less at risk than our analysis assumes. See K. Srinivasan and M. Kachirayan, "Vasectomy Follow-up Study: Findings and Implications," *Institute of Rural Health And Family Planning Bulletin,* 3, No. 1 (July 1968), pp. 20–21. "A Brief Report on the Study of Persons Who have Undergone Vasectomy in the Institute Area," (Mimeographed), Institute of Rural Health and Family Planning, Gandhigram. Other unpublished studies of the Madras vasectomy program have revealed considerably lower levels of abuse than found in the region of Gandhigram.

25. Thomas Poffenberger, "Age of Wives and Number of Living Children of a Sample of Men who Had the Vasectomy in Meerut District, U.P.," *Journal of Family Welfare,* 13, No. 4 (June, 1967), pp. 48–51. These wives of vasectomy cases are slightly older than their counterparts in other regions of India.

26. An even less complicated approach is to assume that a certain percentage of IUD or sterilization adopters would have used the technique even in the absence of the government program. The government program is used only because it is cheaper or more convenient than the private alternative. In this situation, the net impact of the government program is reduced by the percentage of users who had a private alternative.

CHAPTER FOUR

The Economic and Demographic Impact of The Indian Family Planning Program

THE PRESENT relatively short chapter is, in many respects, the heart of the study. It is here that we will attempt to combine the results of the earlier chapters with statistics from the official records to get an economic assessment of the returns to India from past investments in family planning. A bit of history will put the main themes of the chapter in better perspective.

THE HISTORICAL CONTEXT[1]

When the British left India, they did not leave the government with any important role in promulgating birth control—nor is there very much indication that significant proportions of the Indian population were privately practicing modern forms of birth control. The new Indian government, however, was, from the beginning, cognizant of the problems posed by a rapidly increasing population, and in 1952 they initiated the Family Planning Program. The initiation of such a program was a very ambitious undertaking for the newly independent government. No other country had introduced an official policy for the limitation of its population. Thus, there was no example to follow. Moreover, India's immense size and poverty made the task more difficult than it would be in most countries. Public health and medical facilities were inadequate and understaffed, the facilities for communication with much of the population were meager, and the Indian people did not correspond to the experts' notions of a population ready for a breakthrough into birth control.

Under such conditions it was not obvious what would be the best way of attempting to limit population growth. Furthermore, there was a scarcity of the human resources needed for almost any of the approaches that might have been considered. Consequently, the Family Planning Program got off to a slow start,[2] placing most of its emphasis on research and the provision of birth control advice through existing medical facilities. The hope was that eligible couples would respond to the Program by going to the clinics for information and supplies. In the early period the principal method advised was the rhythm method, but it was soon supplemented by foam tablets, condoms, jellies, diaphragms and both male and female sterilization. Thus, the greatest emphasis of the first ten years was on making these clinic services available to as many people as possible. The beginnings of the Program and some aspects of its development are reflected in the record of expenditures on family planning presented in Table IV-1.

By the beginning of the Third Five Year Plan (1961), it was clear that the Program had had little impact during its first years of existence and that the population problem was even more acute than had been recognized earlier. A commission was appointed to review the approach taken by the Ministry

TABLE IV-1

EXPENDITURE ON FAMILY PLANNING PROGRAM
(IN RS. MILLIONS)

Period	Allocation (1)	Actual Expenditure[a] (2)	(2) As Percent of (1) (3)
First Five Year Plan 1951–56	6.5[b]	1.4	21.5%
Second Five Year Plan 1956–61	49.7[b]	21.6	43.5%
Third Five Year Plan 1961–66	270.0[c]	248.6	92.1%
Original Fourth Five Year Plan Draft 1966–71	2,293.1[d]		
Actual Expenditure 1966–69		732.9[e]	
New Fourth Five Year Plan Draft 1969–74	3,000.0[c]		
Final Fourth Five Year Plan 1969–74	3,150.0[f]		

Source:

[a] India, Ministry of Health, Family Planning and Urban Development, Department of Family Planning, "Progress of Family Planning Programme in India," CFPI Reprography Unit, November 1968.

[b] India, Ministry of Health, Directorate General of Health Services, The Central Bureau of Health Intelligence, *Annual Report of the Directorate General of Health Services, 1960*, New Delhi, 1965, p. 180.

[c] India, Planning Commission, *Fourth Five Year Plan 1969–74: Draft*, Delhi, n.d., p. 310–312.

[d] Revised upward from 950.0 million. India, Ministry of Health and Family Planning, *Report 1966–67*, New Delhi, n.d., p. 204.

[e] Expenditure for 1966–69 is estimated. Expenditures for 1968–69 are from the Annual Plan (1969–70), Planning Commission, Government of India as stated in *Economic and Political Weekly*, 5 (Jan. 3, 1970), p. 32.

[f] India, Planning Commission, *Fourth Five Year Plan 1969–74*; Delhi, 1970, p. 393.

of Health and to recommend improvements. The basic change recommended was a switch from the passive clinic approach to an active extension approach.[3] Thus, beginning in 1963, a revised staffing pattern was established, and emphasis was placed on going to the villages to find people interested in family planning.

Further impetus was given to the Program through the introduction of the IUD at the beginning of 1965. It was widely hoped and expected that the technical advantages of the IUD would result in a major breakthrough in family planning in India. Initial acceptance of the IUD was very good, and as will be seen in Table IV-2 and the accompany-

TABLE IV-2

ACCOMPLISHMENTS OF THE FAMILY PLANNING PROGRAM

Year[a]	Sterilizations	IUD Insertions	Condoms Supplied (Millions)	Condom Equivalents[c] (Millions)
1956–57	10,587			
1957–58	16,589		5.8	
1958–59	29,437		4.5	
1959–60	47,881		8.2	
1960–61	74,400		17.1	
1961–62	117,926		26.8	
1962–63	161,022		25.3	
1963–64	195.061		17.2	21.4
1964–65	321,351		47.0	31.6
1965–66	551,007	812,453	52.0	41.9
1966–67	864,237	915,167	31.6	33.5
1967–68	1,840,045	669,208	45.6	27.9
1968–69	1,649,469	472,788	71.3[d]	20.5[d]
1969–70[b]	1,310,744	410,348		

[a] 1956 = January 1, 1956 to March 1, 1957; all other years begin April 1 and end March 31.

[b] 1969–70 is an estimate made by projecting April-December data.

[c] In converting to equivalent condoms, a diaphragm is taken as equal to 36 condoms, one jelly tube equals 72 condoms, one cream tube equals 7 condoms, and one foam tablet equals 1 condom.

[d] Provisional figures. Includes data only up to December.

Source: Sterilization and Insertion data from *Family Planning News*, 8

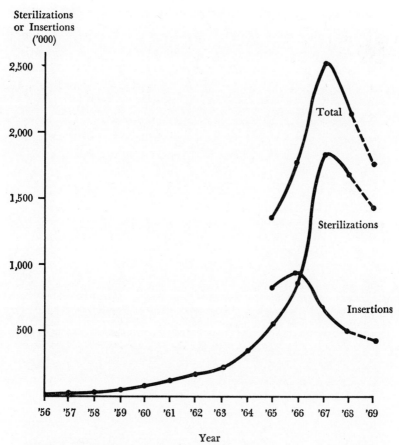

Figure IV-1. Number of Sterilizations and Insertions by Fiscal Year 1956–57 through 1969–70.

(August, 1967), pp. 19–23; 9 (August, 1968), pp. 20–23; 10 (August, 1969), pp. 16–17, and statements I and II, "Monthly Statements on the Progress of Family Planning Programme in India," India, Ministry of Health, Family Planning, Works, Housing and Urban Development, Department of Family Planning, New Delhi, Feb. 10, 1970. Information on condoms and equivalent condoms from "Progress of Family Planning Programme in India," Ministry of Health Family Planning and Urban Development, Department of Family Planning, DFPI Reprography Unit, November, 1968.

ing graph, the number of people coming to the Program for contraceptive assistance expanded dramatically during this period. The high expectations associated with the Family Planning Program during the middle sixties combined with the difficult conditions associated with the droughts of 1965–66 and 1966–67 led planners to dramatically increase the allocations that were assigned to family planning in the Fourth Five Year Plan. The revised plans called for an expansion of program activities in all different directions. Perhaps most important were the suggestions for increasing the extension staff operating from the clinics, reinforcing the administrative capability at all levels and greatly expanding the use of mass media. Despite these changes, the numbers of acceptors seems to have leveled off during the ensuing three years. The most important conclusion to be derived from this brief history is that although progress has been on occasion intermittent and uneven, the Indian government had made a strong and increasing committment to family planning as an important part of the development process. From small and almost symbolic dimensions during the early years, it has become an important element of social and economic policy during recent years.

This capsule history describes some of the characteristics of the Indian investment in family planning in the years since 1952. There has been both a vast expansion in the quantities of resources devoted to the program, and a continuous evolution in the kind of resources being employed. During recent years thousands of buildings have been used in whole or in part for family planning, tens of thousands of workers have been employed in the clinics, and thousands of special research personnel and doctors have worked on various aspects of the Program. Extension workers have made personal visits to millions of families, and their efforts have been complemented by the use of mass media. Our fundamental problem is to discover what has been the impact of all of these activities. It is not easy. These developments did not take place in isolation. Simultaneously there were important changes taking place in many aspects of Indian life. While mortality was declining, the standard of living was slowly rising, and education and urbanization have altered the way of life of many Indians. The thrust of the analysis in the remainder of this chapter is based on the assumption that the impact of the Program can be reasonably represented by the number of sterilizations and IUD insertions and the consequences of these events as derived in Chapters II and III. This assumption will be defended in Chapter V.

PROGRAM RESULTS

In Chapter I, it was suggested that the economic impact of the Family Planning Program can be best measured by the difference between the present value of the economic benefits generated by program activities in any given year and the costs of running the program for that year. In order to estimate the present value of the benefits, it is necessary to establish the number of births prevented by the year in which they were prevented and the present value of the prevented birth. The ground work for the analysis was laid in Chapters II and III. In the present chapter we bring together the results from those chapters and compare the gross benefits thus estimated with the annual expenditures on the Program.

The analysis is based upon the official records of family planning acceptance. Until very recently, the published data for conventional contraceptives has been fragmentary. Consequently, the following discussion is based very largely on the data for sterilization (vasectomy and tubal ligation) and the IUD. These have been the most important contraceptive techniques used by the program, and data concerning their use seems relatively complete. Table IV-2 lists the number of sterilizations and IUD insertions by fiscal year.

It would be very useful to know something of the quality of these statistics. The figures are collected by aggregating at successive levels of administration—clinic, district, state, central government—and there is, a priori, reason to believe that the people doing the compilations might be able to improve their results by adjusting the figures upward. There is almost no evidence on the subject, however, and on the basis of the published evidence there is as much reason to believe the figures correct as to assume that they are inflated.[4] On the other hand, many close observers have pointed out orally that the total number of acceptors is likely to be overstated. Our feeling is that there may well be some inflation in the numbers, but such distortions are not very large. For the moment we will work with the numbers as they are given in the official sources; later in the chapter we will discuss how they can be adjusted if we have some measure of the bias in the statistics.

While it is impossible to give equivalent information regarding the use of ordinary mechanical or chemical contraceptives, such data as exist indicate that there may be a large clientele for the condom, foam, tablets and other contraceptives. The data are given in the form of the number of pieces supplied in a given year, and without a great deal more information, we cannot estimate the number of effective users or of births prevented. Nevertheless, the fact that 45.6 million condoms and 27.9 condom equivalents were supplied in 1967–68 may mean that there were hundreds of thousands of regular users of conventional contraceptives in that year. Since sterilization and the IUD have both a more lasting effect (many women who began using the IUD in 1967–68 are still using it today) and are more effective while in use, a regular user of conventional contraceptives is not likely to have nearly the impact of a sterilization or IUD user. Because of the inadequate information on the users of conventional contraceptives, we will restrict attention in the remainder of our discussion to the IUD and sterilization. Thus, in an important sense we are understating the amount of contraceptive activity in the community.

To develop the analysis any further, it is necessary to translate statistics concerning the number of sterilizations and IUD insertions into the number of births prevented. The fundamental calculations were presented in Chapter III. Under the strong assumption concerning alternative fertility, each insertion was calculated to prevent 0.54 births, and each sterilization 2.35 births .Given these estimates, and given some knowledge concerning the distribution of the prevented births over time (see Tables III-6 and III-13), it is possible to assess the impact of the Program.

An analytical conundrum is created by the fact that Family Planning Program inputs and outputs do not occur simultaneously. Resources used in 1964 may have an impact in 1974. A delayed response may result for three reasons. First, Program activities may cause behavior changes in later years. For example, a couple may resort to sterilization in 1974 because of information gleaned from the educational efforts of 1964. We will ignore this kind of delayed effect. If sterilizations and IUD insertions are assumed to be caused by the activities of the Program, they are associated with expenditures made in the year when they take place. The second kind of delayed Program effect is created by the passage of time between Program expenditure and prevented births. As discussed in Chapter III, a sterilization or an IUD insertion may prevent births many years after it takes place. The third effect was discussed in Chapter II. Once a birth has been prevented the resulting economic benefits may be spread over a number of years. In sum then, ignoring the first type of delayed response, there are two reasons why there may be a delay between expenditures undertaken on family planning and the desired economic effect. In the following section we will discuss the demographic effects of expenditures on family planning. The remainder of the chapter will deal with the economic consequences.

THE EFFECT OF ALL PAST EXPENDITURES
ON THE NUMBER OF BIRTHS
PREVENTED IN A SPECIFIC YEAR

Tables III-6 and III-13 showed the number of births prevented each year according to this analysis after an IUD
insertion or sterilization. The sterilizations which were done
in 1960 will still be preventing births (although a very small
number) in 1985. Likewise the work of 1961 will still be
having a demographic impact in 1986. If we want to know
the number of births prevented in any particular year, say
1970, we must calculate the lagged response to the activities
of each previous year. For example, the impact of the 74,400
sterilizations undertaken in 1960–61 on the number of births
prevented in 1970–71 is found by multiplying by .0911, the
estimate of the number of births prevented in the tenth year
after sterilization (see Table III-13). By repeating this procedure and summing we arrive at an estimate of the total
number of births prevented in 1970. Table IV-3 estimates
the number of births prevented in each year through 1975–
76. It will be noted that by 1964 the number of births prevented was already quite large in absolute terms, and by
1968 it had reached 1,562 thousand.

In Table IV-4 we make a very rough estimate of the Program's impact on the birth rate.[5] If one assumes that the
population is as shown in Column 2, and that the crude
birth rate would have remained constant at 41.7 per thousand (the rate calculated from census returns for the decade
1951–61) in the absence of the Program, then the number
of births taking place each year would be as shown in
Column 3. Column 4 shows the number of births prevented
in each year as estimated in Table IV-3, and Column 5
shows the number of births prevented as a percentage of
the total number of births that would have been expected.
Column 6 shows the crude birth rate which results with the
lower number of births. The results have been projected

TABLE IV-3
NUMBER OF BIRTHS PREVENTED
BY YEAR IN WHICH THEY WOULD HAVE TAKEN PLACE

Fiscal Year Birth is Prevented[a]	Year Sterilization or IUD Insertion Took Place					Total
	Sterilization			IUD Insertion		
	1956–1964	1965–1969	1970–1975[b]	1965–1969	1970–1975[b]	
1956–57	0					0
1957–58	3,747					3,747
1958–59	9,234					9,234
1959–60	18,649					18,649
1960–61	33,489					33,489
1961–62	55,942					55,942
1962–63	91,047					91,047
1963–64	137,117					137,117
1964–65	189,532					189,532
1965–66	279,841	0		0		279,841
1966–67	245,351	195,001		125,036		565,388
1967–68	211,747	480,908		253,613		946,268
1968–69	180,251	1,079,876		302,324		1,562,451
1969–70	152,305	1,542,848		293,489		1,988,642
1970–71	128,055	1,823,695	0	270,408	0	2,222,158
1971–72	108,523	1,591,511	463,872	190,007	63,153	2,417,066
1972–73	93,707	1,364,324	880,295	122,024	120,109	2,580,459
1973–74	79,131	1,154,750	1,246,910	78,448	156,630	2,715,869
1974–75	64,745	973,039	1,562,799	50,477	180,061	2,831,121
1975–76	52,388	826,789	1,831,239	32,444	195,120	2,937,980

[a] Starts April 1.
[b] Projection assuming same annual number of sterilizations (insertions) as in 1969–70.

TABLE IV-4

IMPACT OF THE PROGRAM ON THE BIRTH RATE

Fiscal Year (1)	Populationª (millions) (2)	Birthsᵇ (thousands) in absence of Program (3)	Births (thousands) Prevented Through Programᶜ (4)	(4) as per cent of (3) (5)	Computed CBR with Program (6)
1956–57	399	16,638	0.0	0.00	41.70
1957–58	407	16,972	3.7	.02	41.69
1958–59	415	17,306	9.2	.05	41.68
1959–60	424	17,681	18.6	.11	41.65
1960–61	432	18,014	33.5	.19	41.62
1961–62	443	18,473	55.9	.30	41.57
1962–63	454	18,932	91.0	.48	41.50
1963–64	466	19,432	137.1	.71	41.40
1964–65	477	19,891	189.5	.95	41.30
1965–66	489	20,391	279.8	1.37	41.13
1966–67	501	20,892	565.4	2.71	40.57
1967–68	514	21,434	946.3	4.41	39.86
1968–69	526	21,934	1,562.5	7.12	38.73
1969–70	539	22,476	1,988.6	8.85	38.01
1970–71	553	23,060	2,222.2	9.64	37.68
1971–72	566	23,602	2,417.1	10.24	37.43
1972–73	581	24,228	2,580.5	10.65	37.26
1973–74	595	24,812	2,715.9	10.95	37.13
1974–75	609	25,395	2,831.1	11.15	37.05
1975–76	622	25,937	2,938.0	11.33	36.98

ª Projected backwards and forward from 1967–68 at 2.5 percent per year.
ᵇ Assuming constant crude birth rate (CBR) of 41.7, the rate computed by the Indian Registrar General for 1961 (*Vital Statistics of India for 1961*, p. XLII).
ᶜ 1970–76 projected as in Table IV-3.

forward to 1975–76 on the assumption that the number of sterilizations and IUD insertions would remain constant at the 1969–70 level. According to the exercise then the crude birth rate would decline from the neighborhood of 41.7 in the late fifties to 38.0 in 1969–70 and further to 37.0 in 1975–76. However, even a number of that size is small compared to the huge number of births taking place each year in India (Column 3 of Table IV-4). One should not attach too much significance to the result. The exercise is only meant to give an order of magnitude. The percentage reduction in the birth rate is so small that it might well not be noticed, or could be largely or completely offset by fertility-raising factors associated with declining mortality.

The second draft of the Fourth Five Year Plan suggests that

> In order to make economic development yield tangible benefits for the ordinary people, it is necessary that the birth rate be brought down substantially as early as possible. It is proposed to aim at a reduction of this rate from 39 per thousand to 25 per thousand population within the next 10–12 years.[6]

However imperfect the results of the exercise reported in Table IV-4, it should be clear that the Indian Family Planning Program must be much more effective before it can reach its targets. George Stolnitz has estimated in a recent paper that for India to achieve its family planning targets nearly all fecund couples where the wife is 25 or older would have to accept family planning by the end of the period mentioned.[7] There are currently 78.8 million married women between 15 and 44, of whom 49.3 million are older than 25. About 3.5 million women join the eligible group each year.[8] Thus if the Program is to make a significant inroad in this huge number of eligible couples, the number of acceptors should be much larger than it has been during the past few years. Clearly, the impact of the Program on the number of births taking place in any given year has been rather limited up to the present, but there has been a start and, as we will attempt to show below, the economic return on the investments to the present make the effort very worthwhile.

THE ECONOMICS OF THE INDIAN INVESTMENT IN FAMILY PLANNING

The remainder of this chapter examines the economics of the Indian investment in family planning. We will just examine the costs of the program and then compare them with the economic benefits that are generated.

The cost of the Family Planning Program

All of the activities undertaken as a part of the Indian investment in Family Planning have costs. In an ideal investment situation the costs of the Program would be represented by the actual amounts of money spent on the various inputs to the Program. In a situation as complex as that associated with the Indian Family Planning Program, it may be more appropriate to imagine costs in the sense of lost opportunities. The use of resources in family planning means that those same resources cannot be used for other purposes. A vehicle used to transport family planning workers cannot be used to carry engineers working at a dam site. Doctors who spend full time on family planning do so at the expense of their more immediate curative tasks. The difficulty with using the opportunity-cost approach to measuring Program inputs is that it is not entirely clear what is the value of inputs in various alternatives. The problem can be demonstrated by examining the use of human inputs into the Program. A large proportion of Program expenditures are for various kinds of personnel.[9] In India many educated people are unemployed. Thus the most likely alternative for many of the men and women employed as extension workers is unemployment. If this is the case, their wages may overstate the social cost of their services. On the other hand, trained doctors are very scarce, and there may be very heavy opportunity costs to using their time in family planning. In sum it seems almost impossible to strike a balance on whether the expenditures on family planning represent the true social cost of the Program. We will assume that they do.

Having decided to use expenditures in the Program as a measure of costs we face a problem in discovering exactly what have been the expenditures. There are several sources which present expenditure series. There are a number of points of detail upon which they differ.[10] For our purposes we have chosen to use the series presented in the official government statistics.

Economic Benefits

There is a double lag between expenditures on family planning and the benefits which they generate. Both lags can be dealt with through the device of discounted present values. In Chapter II, we attempted to make a reasonable estimate of the value of preventing a birth in 1967–68. For the analysis of this section we will assume that the estimate of Rs. 7,800 from Example III can be applied to all years— both before and after 1967–68. This assumption obviously adds some distortions; since the value of a birth prevented depends on per capita income in the base year, the value of preventing a birth before 1967–68 is overstated and that for later years is understated. Fortunately the error introduced in this manner is not very large. The assertion that the value of a prevented birth is constant facilitates the estimation of the overall economic effect of the program.

As an intermediate step it is useful to estimate the present value of a sterilization or an IUD insertion.

$$\text{P.V. (sterilization in Year 0)} = \sum_{t=0}^{n} \frac{\text{PVBP}_t \cdot \text{BP}_t}{(1+i)^t}$$

where PVBP_t = the present value of preventing a birth in year t after the year in which the sterilization is performed.

BP_t = the number of births prevented in year t by the sterilization in year zero.

n = the last year in which births can be assumed to be prevented by a sterilization.

i = the rate of discount.

t = number of years elapsed since sterilization or IUD insertion.

In the following tables we have assumed that $PVBP_t$ = Rs. 7,800, and i = 10 percent, and BP_t is taken from the appropriate table of Chapter III. The number which results from this procedure is the present value of the stream of benefits resulting from a sterilization. It has, in turn, been multiplied by the number of sterilizations taking place in any given year to give the present value of the benefits from all the sterilizations of that year. An analogous procedure is used to estimate the present value of the benefits generated by the IUD insertions taking place in any given year.

THE BALANCE BETWEEN COSTS AND BENEFITS

Table IV-5 presents an estimate of the benefits generated by the activities of the Indian Family Planning Program during each year from 1956–57 through 1969–70. The underlying present value of a sterilization is Rs. 11,562 and of an IUD insertion is Rs. 3,243. The total gross benefits generated by the activities of any given year are presented in Column 7. They can be compared with the annual expenditures as given in Column 2. The total net benefits—i.e., the difference between Column 7 and Column 2—is given in Column 8 and the ratio of benefits to costs is shown in Column 9. The ratio of benefits to costs is very high. For 1967–68 it is 88:1.

There are two lessons that might be drawn from Table IV-5. First, the economic return on the money invested in the Family Planning Program has already been quite high. Often the unimpressive impact of the Program on the total rate of population growth makes one forget that the per-

TABLE IV-5
ANNUAL EXPENDITURE AND RETURN ON FAMILY PLANNING INVESTMENT

Fiscal Year[a] (1)	Expenditure During Year (million 1967–68 Rs) (2)	Sterilizations During Year (thousands) (3)	Present Value of Sterilizations (million 1967–68 Rs) (4)	IUD's Inserted (thousands) (5)	Present Value of IUD's Inserted (million 1967–68 Rs) (6)	Total Gross Benefits from Program (million 1967–68 Rs) (7)	Total Benefits from Program (7)–(2) (8)	Ratio of Return to Expenditure (9)
1956-57	1.74	10.6	122.6			122.6	120.9	70.5
1957-58	4.91	16.6	191.9			191.9	187.0	39.1
1958-59	5.63	29.4	339.9			339.9	334.3	60.4
1959-60	8.79	47.9	553.8			553.8	545.0	63.0
1960-61	16.68	74.4	860.2			860.2	843.5	51.6
1961-62	23.22	117.9	1363.2			1363.2	1340.0	58.7
1962-63	44.71	161.0	1861.5			1861.5	1861.8	41.6
1963-64	33.94	195.0	2254.6			2254.6	2220.7	66.4
1964-65	90.60	321.4	3716.0			3716.0	3625.4	41.0
1965-66	151.90	551.0	6370.7	812.5	2635.0	9005.0	8853.1	59.3
1966-67	152.05	864.2	9991.9	915.2	2968.0	12959.9	12807.8	85.2
1967-68	265.30	1840.0	21274.1	669.2	2170.2	23444.3	23179.0	88.4
1968-69	324.08	1649.5	19071.6	472.8	1533.3	20604.9	20280.8	63.6
1969-70	406.80	1310.7	15154.3	410.3	1330.6	16484.9	16078.1	40.5

[a] Starts April 1.

Source: Data for 1956–68 from India, Ministry of Health, Family Planning and Urban Development, Department of Family Planning, "Progress of Family Planning Programme in India," CFPI Reprography Unit, Nov. 1968. Data for 1968–70 from Annual Plan (1969–70), Planning Commission, Government of India as stated in Economic and Political Weekly, 5 (Jan. 3, 1970), p. 32.

centage decline in the birth rate is not the only measure of the Program's success. Second, the very high ratio of benefits to costs indicates that the marginal return is in all likelihood much higher than the marginal cost, and there is strong justification for expanding the Program as rapidly as is humanly possible. The object of the planner is not just to maximize the return on investments; it is to maximize the total welfare of the population.

It should be noted that the benefit-cost ratio is proportionate to the value of preventing a birth, to the number of births prevented per insertion or sterilization, and to the number of sterilizations and IUD insertions that take place. Consequently, the final figure for the benefits or for the benefit-cost ratio can be adjusted to match any set of expectations concerning the "true" values of these important parameters. Thus, if the reader feels that the value of preventing a birth is only Rs. 3,900 (or half of the Rs. 7,800 value used in the calculations), he can adjust the figure downward by dividing by two. Each of the annual benefit-cost ratios would then be halved. Similarly, if the assumptions used in Chapter III regarding alternative fertility are judged to be too optimistic, the benefit figure can be adjusted downward. For example, if, in the absence of the Program, one-third of the adoptors would have used contraceptive techniques as effective as the IUD or sterilization that they actually used, then the figure for the benefits should be reduced by one third. An analogous adjustment can be made for distortions in the official statistics. These simple relationships make adjustments easy, but we will argue in the next chapter that the values actually given are reasonable estimates of the benefits from the Indian investment in family planning.

Most of the benefits resulting from the activities of the Indian Family Planning Program are delayed. But the benefits which the Program generates are so large that the initial costs are repaid in short order. Table IV-6 shows the benefits which accrue in each year as a result of all previous activity in family planning. This table makes it clear that India is already enjoying the benefits of past expenditures in family planning. Since its impact is relatively diffused, the Family Planning Program does not have results which are dramatically obvious. Nevertheless, the desired effects of the Program develop rapidly.

TABLE IV-6

BENEFITS ACCRUING IN A YEAR AS THE RESULT OF BIRTHS
PREVENTED IN ALL PRECEDING YEARS AND ANNUAL
TOTAL EXPENDITURE ON THE PROGRAM (MILLION 1967–68 RS.)

Fiscal Year[a]	Benefits	Expenditures[b]	Benefit/ Expenditure
1956–57	.0	1.74	.0
1957–58	.0	4.91	.0
1958–59	1.94	5.63	.34
1959–60	6.66	8.79	.76
1960–61	16.26	16.68	.97
1961–62	33.65	23.22	1.45
1962–63	62.96	44.71	1.41
1963–64	111.09	33.94	3.27
1964–65	184.25	90.60	2.03
1965–66	286.75	151.90	1.89
1966–67	439.69	152.05	2.89
1967–68	745.61	265.30	2.81
1968–69	1254.58	324.08	3.87
1969–70	2096.11	406.80[c]	5.15
1970–71	3180.98		
1971–72	4431.10		
1972–73	5847.24		
1973–74	7429.41		
1974–75	9180.25		
1975–76	11107.48		

[a] Starts April 1.
[b] Source: Data for 1956–68 from India, Ministry of Health, Family Planning and Urban Development, Department of Family Planning, "Progress of Family Planning Programme in India," CFPI Reprography Unit, November 1968. Data for 1968–70 from Annual Plan (1969–70), Planning Commission, Government of India as stated in *Economic and Political Weekly*, 5 (Jan. 3, 1970), p. 32.
[c] Budgeted

Table IV-7 summarizes many of the findings of this chapter for one year—1967–68. The expenditures on family planning during the year were quite large, but the activities of the Program managed to generate a large return—sufficient to repay the original investment within 2.7 years. The average cost of recruiting a family planning acceptor was relatively high—Rs. 106—but the calculations indicate that the expenditure was well justified.

TABLE IV-7

THE PROGRAM IN 1967–68

Expenditure:	265.3 mill. Rs.
Sterilizations:	1,840,000
Insertions:	669,200
Cost per acceptor of sterilization or insertion:	105.7 Rs.
Total births averted:	4,683,077
Cost per birth averted:	56.65 Rs.
Present value of benefits through 1992–93 from births averted:	23,444.3 Mill. Rs.
Period necessary for recovery of 1967–68 outlays ("pay back" period):	2.7 years
Benefits/Cost:	88.4

NOTES

1. There are a number of sources that describe the history of the Indian Family Planning Program. Three of the more useful are S. N. Agarwala, *Population* (New Delhi: National Book Trust, 1967), Chapters XIII-XIV; Raina, "India," pp. 111–121; S. Chandrasekhar, "How India Is Tackling her Population Problem," *Foreign Affairs*, 47 (October, 1968), pp. 138–150; and Moye W. Freymann, "India's Family Planning Program: Some Lessons Learned," in *Population Dynamics*, edited by Minoru Muramatsu and Paul A. Harper, pp. 13–26, (Baltimore: The Johns Hopkins Press, 1965).

2. Given the circumstances, the slow start is understandable, but, in many respects, a reasonably impartial observer might have hoped

for a more rapid response. See Chapter VIII for a discussion of some possible reasons for the slow beginning.

3. See Raina, *Family Planning Programme Report for 1962–63*; and Nicholas J. Demerath, "Family Planning: Plans and Action," *The Journal of Public Administration*, 11 (October–December, 1965), pp. 683–697.

4. See Simmons, "The Indian Investment in Family Planning," Chapter X, p. 185. It is important to note that there may be under-recording in some instances, especially during the early period when targets and incentives played a smaller role than they do presently.

4. S. P. Jain makes similar estimates of the demographic impact of the Program. His methodology differs from that used here, but the results are somewhat similar, "Estimation of Population Growth under Family Planning Programme," *Journal of Family Welfare*, 16, No. 1 (Sept. 1969), pp. 33–47.

6. India, Planning Commission, *Fourth Five Year Plan 1969–74: Draft*, New Delhi, 1969.

7. George J. Stolnitz, "Estimating the Birth Effects of India's Family Planning Targets: A Report on Statistical Methodology and Illustrative Projections, 1968–78," mimeograph (July–August, 1968), p. 21.

8. Of course the number of eligible couples is also reduced each year by death and aging.

9. See for example Warren Robinson *et al.*, "A Cost-Effectiveness Analysis of Selected National Family Planning Programs: A Report on Phase II of the Penn State-USAID Population Project 'Cost-Benefit and Cost-Effectiveness Evaluation of Family Planning Programs,'" Pennsylvania State University, Dept. of Economics, December 1969, Tables VI and VII.

10. India, Ministry of Health, Family Planning and Urban Development, Department of Family Planning, "Progress of Family Planning Programme in India," CFPI Reprography Unit, November, 1968. Also in United Nations, Commissioner for Technical Cooperation, Department of Economic and Social Affairs, "An Evaluation of the Family Planning Programme of The Government of India," Oct. 13, 1969, p. 11, and "India: The Family Planning Programme since 1965," *Studies in Family Planning*, 35 (Nov., 1968), pp. 6–7. A study group from Pennsylvania State University have also made estimates of the expenditures on family planning. See Robinson *et al.*, "A Cost-Effectiveness Analysis of Selected National Family Planning Programs."

CHAPTER FIVE

Can The Prevention of Births in India Be Attributed to The Government Investment in Family Planning?

MUCH OF THE ANALYSIS of the previous chapters hinges on the assumption that government investments in family planning were a necessary condition for the prevention of births. We have assumed that if adoptors had not used the IUD or sterilization, their fertility would have been the same as that of noncontracepting women of similar fecundity in the same age class. This is to say, in the absence of the government Family Planning Program, the adoptors would not have reduced their fertility. This assumption is debatable, for, as mentioned earlier, many changes have taken place in Indian society that may have had an impact on fertility, and we cannot attribute the benefits of birth prevention to government investments unless we can demonstrate that such investments were necessary for fertility reduction.

Before proceeding with the argument, it is important to give at least passing attention to the interpretation of causality that is being used here. There are two levels on which one can interpret a casual relationship to exist between family planning investments and the economic benefits resulting from decreased population growth. First, we might say that the existence of the Family Planning Program caused a reduction in fertility because the people who adopted the IUD or sterilization received their treatment from the doctors and paramedical staff working for the Program. In the strictest sense, this is accurate because, for the most part, these treatments are only available through the government-sponsored clinics and hospitals. However, a broader interpretation of causality is in order here. The larger issue is how many births would take place with and without the facilities for IUD insertion and sterilization provided by the government. The question is not whether the IUD insertions and sterilizations were done by the employees of the Program, but what the acceptors of these services would have done if such convenient services had not been provided by the government.

An important implication follows from the above interpretation. We are examining the influence that the existence of investments in family planning has upon fertility behavior. There are, of course, many factors that affect fertility, but we are concerned with the net additional change induced by government activity. Thus, the possibility that the couples using the IUD or sterilization might come from those groups in society most favorably inclined toward fertility control would not affect the contribution that we are crediting to the Program, unless the group in question would have reduced its fertility autonomously. If the existence of the Program means that the acceptors will be able to prevent births that would otherwise occur, then the economic benefits flowing from the prevented births are considered to be its creation. To repeat, then, the central question of this chapter is whether the various clinical services and other Program activities were *necessary* for the results discussed in Chapter IV. It is not relevant to ask whether those investments were a *sufficient* condition for birth prevention. It might well be that other changes in Indian society have helped to increase the response to the Program to a level greatly in excess of what it would have been ten years ago. Certainly there have been many factors influencing the responses of acceptors, but our primary concern is to determine the marginal contribution of the Program.[1]

We are not attempting to rule out the use of contraception independent of the Program. Even without the Program there are undoubtedly millions of families who have made efforts to restrict their fertility. Indian fertility is not at the physiological maximum; consequently indigenous methods of fertility control within marriage must exist and have existed for many years. We are seeking only to establish whether there are plausible reasons for believing that those couples who have used the IUD or sterilization would not have obtained equivalent protection in the absence of the Program. There are undoubtedly many couples who use contraceptives which they have obtained from non-governmental sources. Many are motivated by factors having nothing whatever to do with the Program, and many others are using contraception because of the educational efforts of the Program.

The fertility decline which has taken place in Europe, the countries of European extraction, and Japan was not accompanied by government programs for population limitation. Fertility decreased despite the lack of government involvement. There are some generalizations that can be made, however, about the experiences of these countries.[2] A fairly long period of substantial and sustained economic and social change preceded the decline in most of the countries. In every case there was a decline in mortality prior to any decline in fertility. The mechanism by which the changes in the social environment were translated into fertility decline are not completely clear, but it has been hypothesized that the fertility decline was a response to the new environment created by the decline in mortality and the progress in the social and economic spheres.

> My thesis is that, faced with a persistent high rate of natural in-crease resulting from past success in controlling mortality, families tended to use every demographic means possible to maximize their new opportunities and to avoid relative loss of status. . . . If each family is concerned with its prospective standing in comparison to other families within its reference group, we can understand why the peoples of the industrializing and hence prospering coun-tries altered their demographic behavior in numerous ways that had the effect of reducing the population growth brought about by lowered mortality.[3]

The movement in the Western countries was led by those segments of society whose positions were the most affected by the changes taking place in the society at large. The first contraceptors tended to be the better-educated, urban-dwell-ing, upwardly mobile, middle-class families who were pressed by their social position to limit the size of their families. To maintain a familiar standard of living and to assure an ade-quate education for their children, this middle class was willing to use unaccustomed measures that often entailed considerable inconvenience and possibly moral introspec-tion. Eventually, most groups followed the example of the first adoptors.[4]

The preceding paragraph describes briefly the paradigm created for India by those countries that have already ex-perienced fertility decline. There is at least one element in the Indian situation that did not exist in the other countries —the government-sponsored Family Planning Program, the existence of which offers an opportunity for couples, who would otherwise have used other channels, to take advantage of free and effective contraceptive services. If such couples represent the bulk of the users of sterilization and the IUD in India, then we would expect their numbers and socio-economic characteristics to be somewhat similar to the pattern established by the other countries. That is, the first Indian adoptors should be responding to the same kind of fundamental changes in the conditions of life that took place in the other countries, and it should be those couples who are most exposed to the challenge of social change who are most ready to respond. If, on the other hand, the bulk of the acceptors can be said to have been brought to the use of effective contraception by the Program, then we would expect that the initial contraceptive use would begin before mortality and social and economic development had progressed to the level achieved at the time of fertility reduction in the low-fertility countries, and that the early acceptors would differ from their Western analogues.

Our basic argument in this chapter is that, although there has been considerable social change in India in recent years, it has not been of the magnitude of that which preceded sustained fertility decline in other countries. Furthermore, the adoptors of the IUD and sterilization are not representative of the class that one might expect to initiate fertility decline. Finally, interregional variations in the rates of acceptance seem to be explained better by the size of inputs into the Program than by variations in existing social conditions.

*

SOCIAL CHANGE IN INDIA AND THE DEMOGRAPHIC TRANSITION

The Indian Family Planning Program has not been introduced into an otherwise stable social and economic environment. Many other changes relevant to reproductive behavior have either developed autonomously or have resulted from government programs of various kinds. Of the many changes taking place, three merit particular attention: (1) the decline in mortality, (2) the increase in the educated and/or urban segment of the population, and (3) the slow, but continuing transformation of the Indian economy. These developments are of particular interest because similar changes preceded or accompanied the decline in fertility in the countries of Europe and in Japan.

In India the expectation of life at birth for males has increased from less than twenty-five years during the first two decades of this century to somewhere in excess of forty-five years during the past few years.[5] Mortality in India has thus declined to a level approaching the levels existing in European countries when fertility began to decline. The decline of mortality has fundamentally altered the decision-making environment for parents. Where once the average parents could only expect to replace themselves, today there is the possibility of doubling the entire population within the reproductive span of a single mother. This, in turn, implies a doubling of the number of people requiring land and employment. Consequently, when parents realize the implications of the new mortality conditions, they will recognize that they can achieve the traditional expectations of the number of children surviving to adulthood with fewer births. They will also become aware that there are penalities for having many more children than are needed to replace themselves. There may be some offsetting advantages of a large family, but the key point is that the new mortality conditions will alter the framework in which the decisions are made.

The decline of mortality in India has, however, been much more rapid than it was in the European countries, and it is not clear how long it will take for the population to react to the changes.[6] The history of mortality decline in Latin America suggests that when mortality declines very rapidly, it may have to decline farther than it did in Europe before there is a response in the level of fertility. Thus even if the mortality level in India is now roughly comparable with levels prevailing in the West when the fertility decline began, any possible decline in India may have to wait either for the passage of a number of years or a further decline in mortality. Moreover, the decline in Europe and Japan was accompanied by fundamental alterations in the economy of a kind that have not taken place in India.

The continuing spread of education and the relative growth of the cities are additional factors that may be working to alter the decision-making framework of parents. More children have been attending schools during recent years than in pre-Independence India, and general literacy has increased from 16.6 percent of the population in 1951 to 24 percent in 1961.[7] During the same period the proportion of the population living in the cities increased slightly from 17.35 percent in 1951 to 17.97 percent in 1961.

These developments are important. Education and exposure to a different way of life in the city represent a break with tradition, and there is hope that this will lead eventually to a desire for fewer children and a greater awareness of the possibility of controlling the number of births. It should be noted that the absolute levels of literacy and urbanization in India are still very low—lower than they were in most of the other countries that have completed the demographic transition. If the historical pattern were to be repeated, a sustained fertility decline would have to wait for more significant change in these areas. The rapid rise in population is itself a reason why increases in education and urbanization are slow in coming.

The evidence indicates that the standard of living in India has improved very slowly over the last twenty years. After thirty years of stagnation,[8] per capita income increased by about 20 percent between 1948–49 and the late nineteen-sixties. The per capita availability of food has increased very little since independence. The question here, as above, is how much should one expect the standard of living to increase before there would be an autonomous decline in fertility? Basically, despite recent improvements, India is still poorer than were other countries when the latter began to experience a decline in fertility. There has been a slight improvement in per capita income. The question is whether such a change is sufficient or whether one must wait for per capita income to double or quadruple before there will be an autonomous decline in fertility.

In sum, then, the history of recent social and economic change is not very hopeful. There has been a decline in fertility and some social and economic progress, but these changes are not yet of the magnitude that would indicate a rapid reduction in fertility.[9] If continued at the recent pace, such changes might be expected to bring about the conditions for a fertility decline within the next few decades, but if an autonomous decline were to set in under existing conditions, India would be unique. The other countries that have undergone the demographic transition were all more advanced in both the social and the economic areas before the change set in. That is, in the area of mortality, India has just crossed the threshold into the levels of expectation of life at birth that existed in other countries at the time of fertility decline, and by no other measure have the preconditions for a decline in fertility been established.

SOCIAL CHARACTERISTICS
OF INDIVIDUAL ADOPTORS

We argued in the previous section that social and economic conditions in India have not yet reached the stage where we would expect fertility to decline of its own accord. If acceptors of the IUD and sterilization represented the beginnings of a demographic transition, we would expect that members of the most advanced social classes would be over-represented. Moreover we would not expect extension workers employed by the Program to play a major role in recruitment. Unfortunately, there are no statistics for the national program which can be used to test these hypotheses. In their absence we must resort to isolated studies of particular regions. Most of these studies do not include information about the general population from which acceptors were drawn. Thus it is difficult to make strong statements concerning the differences between those people who accept and those who do not accept the family planning services offered by the Program.

Ideally we would have sufficient information to indicate whether there are different response rates among social groups that have had the same exposure to the Program. if the more educated, better off, urban groups were the only respondents we might then conclude that it was only the most motivated groups that responded to the Program and further that these people are sufficiently motivated that they would have used effective contraception whether or not the government had made its large investment in family planning. In the present section we examine evidence from a number of studies from different regions in India. We argue that: (1) the first acceptors of the IUD and sterilization are not drawn predominantly from any social class that one might expect to be more exposed to social change than others, and (2) most of the cases were actively recruited by extension workers. Such evidence would seem to be consistent with the hypothesis that these couples would not have been able to reduce their fertility effectively in the absence of the government efforts in family planning.[10]

In Haryana,[11] adoptors of the IUD differed from women in the general population by their high age and parity. There was also a tendency for adoptors to be slightly more educated than nonadoptors, but it is notable that 82 percent of the women interviewed were illiterate. Thus, while education seems to be correlated with IUD acceptance, such acceptance is by no means restricted to the most educated groups in the community. All of the IUD's used by the women interviewed in Haryana were inserted by the staff of the government health service. When the women were asked how they had first heard about the IUD, 85 percent named a government extension worker. The responses from one of the districts studied indicated that in 43 percent of the cases, government workers had been most responsible for convincing the respondent to adopt the IUD. About one-third of the respondents had tried some method of family planning before the insertion of the IUD, but most of these women had used devices supplied by the Primary Health Centers. Thus, it would seem fair to conclude that most women studied would not have used any method of preventing further pregnancies had it not been for the existence of the government Program. The women are not part of an unusually advanced class; their uniqueness is derived from their relatively high parities, and their use of contraception was, in almost all cases, associated with the government extension program and with the existence of government clinics.

The situation is similar with regard to the Program in other areas of India. In Madras the extension work for the relatively successful program of sterilization is done by "canvassers"—individuals, sterilized themselves, who are paid ten rupees for each case they bring to the hospitals equipped to do sterilization. Of the 1,000 vasectomy cases from Madras City reported on by R. A. Krishnan, 57 percent said their monthly income was less than Rs. 50, meaning that the majority of the sample of vasectomized heads of households had incomes well below the national average.[12] Nearly 45 percent of the sample was illiterate, as compared with the 30 percent rate of illiteracy reported by the 1961 Census for Madras City. Finally, 98.7 percent of the sample reported that they were brought for the vasectomy operation by the government field workers. It is probably fair to conclude that the people who have been sterilized in Madras City are relatively poor and badly educated. In no sense are they an **elite group.**

Information concerning the characteristics of sterilization cases has been collected by one of the "Action Research Programs" in rural Kerala.[13] There, researchers studied a large sample taken randomly from the general population of married women in the fertile age groups. Among the 1,781 women interviewed, 271 had been "effectively" sterilized (i.e., either the husband or the wife had been sterilized). The sterilized women differed from the nonsterilized in that they were older and of higher parity. But there is no significant difference in the distribution of the two groups by income or monthly expenditure. Sterilized couples tend to be less educated and to come from nuclear, as opposed to extended, family situations, but since neither of these relationships is standardized for age, the significance of the finding is not clear. As in the other examples presented, however, it is clear that the sterilized couples do not represent any particular class.

A somewhat similar study undertaken in a moderately affluent section of Calcutta provides interesting information. In this study a general sample was drawn from the population. Among the couples interviewed there were both users and non-users of contraception (largely the condom and non-device methods). Two points emerge from the study. First, contraceptors tend to be slightly more educated than non-contraceptors. Among users, the higher the educational attainment the more likely it is that the couple resorted to sources of supply other than the Health Center. Thus, on balance, the study indicates that the users of government family planning services tend to be fairly representative of the population at risk.[14]

Despite the fact that there have been many other studies of family planning acceptors[15] we are still relatively ignorant concerning the factors which differentiate acceptors and non-acceptors. From the very limited information that is available, it would seem that acceptors are differentiated largely by the number of children (especially sons) living in the family. Since a large proportion of acceptors were actively recruited by persons employed by the Program, it is likely that they have been more exposed to Program contacts than have non-acceptors. There is no firm evidence for this hypothesis, since we do not know how much contact non-acceptors have had with the Program. There is a slight tendency for acceptors to be better educated than non-acceptors. Most of the studies of acceptors[16] present less evidence as to the social class and the nature of Program contacts than do those discussed above, but the conclusions are similar. The people coming to the government family planning clinics are from all classes, and there is usually a direct link between acceptance and the efforts of the Program extension staff.

THE EVIDENCE FROM AGGREGATE DATA

In order to test some of the hypotheses concerning the determinants of family planning acceptance, data from 246 districts in India have been analyzed to isolate those factors which are most strongly associated with the acceptance of the IUD and sterilization during 1966. If there is, indeed, a causal relationship between the government program and acceptance, as measured by the ratio of acceptors to total population, then we would expect to find a statistically significant association between acceptance and variables measuring the program inputs. Alternatively, if it is the level of development that explains acceptance, then one would expect that socioeconomic variables explain most of the variation in acceptance rates and that policy variables are statistically insignificant. It should be noted that the unit of analysis in this case is the district (a social aggregate) and not the individual. Consequently, our conclusions can be generalized to individual behavior only with a great deal of caution.

The data used for the analysis are inadequate in a number of ways. District data from IUD or sterilization acceptance are lacking for the districts of two of the major states.[17]

More important, the data concerning Program inputs are limited to the number of clinics operating in each district and, for a smaller number of districts, the number of extension workers in the field. There are no data for the quality of the organization or the level of training of the people working for the Program in any given district. Socioeconomic data are more complete, thanks to the extensive tabulations of the 1961 Census. Table V-1 shows the distribution of the 246 districts by acceptance rates. It will be noted that very few of the districts had acceptance rates above 15 per thousand. Of course the total number of users in a district could be higher, but the general level of acceptance is quite low.

The basic measure of acceptance which we have used in the analysis is the ratio of the number of acceptors of either sterilization or the IUD to the total population living in the district at the time of the 1961 Census. This measure of response is probably a reasonable operational goal used by program administrators. It differs from the measure of out-

TABLE V-1

THE DISTRIBUTION OF DISTRICTS BY
FAMILY PLANNING ACCEPTANCE DURING 1966

Acceptance Index (IUD insertions and sterilizations/1000 pop.)	Number of Districts	Percent of Districts
0.0– 1.0	28	11.4
1.0– 2.5	79	32.1
2.5– 5.0	53	21.6
5.0– 7.5	34	13.8
7.5–10.0	17	6.9
10.0–15.0	13	5.3
15.0+	22	8.9
	246	100.0

Source: data for 246 districts provided by Ministry of Health and Family Planning, New Delhi.

put (the economic benefits from birth prevention) which we have ourselves employed in the earlier chapters.

The number of clinics operating in a given district is the only measure of Program inputs available for all 246 districts under study. This number can be taken as a very crude proxy for the amount of quantitative input into the Program. The main purpose of the clinics is to distribute medical services associated with family limitation and to serve as the base of extension work conducted in the surrounding areas. Eventually the government hopes to have a clinic for every 80,000 population in the rural areas and for every 45,000 in the urban areas, but as of 1966 there was considerable variation in the ratio of clinics to population. For lack of more adequate information, the clinic-to-population ratio can be thought of as a measure of the intensity of the services to the community living in the district.

For a smaller number of districts, information is available concerning the number of extension workers employed in each.[18] The extension worker/population ratio is a reasonable measure of the quantity of work that is being done in any given district, but not of the quality. On the whole, however, it is probably a better measure of Program effort than the clinic/population ratio.

Three different measures of socioeconomic development have been used in the analysis. The first is the percentage of the population that is literate.[19] This is a measure of the receptiveness to different sources of information. Generally it is regarded by social scientists as an important index of social development.

The second variable used is urbanization,[20] the proportion of the residents in any district who live in communities classed as urban. In India a community is normally classified as urban if its population exceeds 5,000 persons. There are exceptions for smaller communities with some urban characteristics and for communities which, despite the size of their population, are rural in character. Urbanization is again one of the major indices of social development. The different living styles of village and town may make themselves felt in numerous aspects of individual behavior. The urbanization variable can be hypothesized to have two effects on family planning acceptance. First, urban residents may be more disposed to accept family planning. Second, it may be easier to operate a program in the urban environment where supporting services (e.g., hospitals, relatively developed communication and transportation systems) are more available than they are in the rural areas.

The final variable which has been used is the per capita income of the residents of the districts.[21] The per capita income data refers to 1955–1956 and is thus outdated, but it probably does give a fair index of the relative incomes of the different districts. The means and standard deviations for all of the variables are shown in Table V-2.

Table V-3 shows the statistical results of regressing each of the independent variables on our measure of family planning acceptance. It is assumed that there is a linear relation-

TABLE V-2

MEAN VALUES AND STANDARD DEVIATIONS FOR THE
VARIABLES USED IN DISTRICT ANALYSIS

Variable	246 Districts		56 Districts	
	Mean	S.D.	Mean	S.D.
IUD's inserted in 1966	2844	3336	3009	2319
Sterilizations in 1966	2095	2829	1692	1671
Urban clinics in 1966	3.923	6.670	3.357	3.305
Rural clinics in 1966	15.508	9.626	15.21	5.83
Extension workers in 1966	—	—	95.18	93.59
Population divided by 100	13621	9257.6	9667.2	7850.8
Number literate per 1000 Population	233.6	100.2	250.0	124.36
Number urban per 1000 Population	171.69	151.96	171.27	99.9
Per capita income 1955–56 (rupees)	221.13	76.878	233.0	48.01
(Acceptors/population) × 100	.667	1.132	.7618	.6488
(Clinics/population) × 100	.00304	.00486	.0073	.0079
(Extension workers/population) × 100	—	—	.0113	.0085

ship among the variables. When all of the 246 districts with complete data are used in the regression, each of the four independent variables is by itself significantly (at 95 percent) related to family planning acceptance (see Equations 1-3 and 5). The variable which is most strongly correlated with family planning acceptance is the clinic/population ratio, but literacy and urbanization are also strongly associated with family planning acceptance. The measure of per capita income is significantly related to acceptance, but the correlation is low.

When the independent variables are used together the amount of variation explained increases, thus implying that both the clinic/population ratio and the socioeconomic variables contribute to family planning acceptance. Literacy is significantly associated with acceptance, but again it is the clinic/population ratio which shows the strongest impact on acceptance. This result is especially clear in equation 9 where all of the independent variables are regressed simultaneously on family planning acceptance. It should be noted that the amount of explained variation in family planning acceptance rates never exceeds 22 percent. Clearly there are factors involved in exploring the acceptance rates which have not been introduced into the analysis.

By using a more refined measure of program input—the ratio of extension workers to population—for the smaller sample of districts, we are able to explain a larger amount of the variation in family planning acceptance. Such data is available only for the districts in Kerala, Maharashtra and Rajasthan. When all five of the independent variables which we have used in the analysis of the smaller number of districts are included the percentage of the variance explained rises to 54 percent. The clinic/population ratio is still the most powerful explanatory variable when each of the independent variables is associated singly with family planning acceptance, but the extension worker/population ratio is nearly as highly correlated. Each of the two is much more highly correlated with acceptance than is any of the socioeconomic variables. It is interesting that for the 56 districts in the small sample the correlation between the clinic/population ratio and the extension worker/population ratio is relatively low, $r = .23$ (see Table V-4). When the two meas-

TABLE V-3
THE CORRELATES OF FAMILY PLANNING ACCEPTANCE[a]
(PARTIAL CORRELATION COEFFICIENTS)

Equation Number	Literacy	Urbanization	Per Capita Income	Clinics/ Population	Workers/ Population	R^2
			246 Districts			
1	.26					.07
2		.33				.11
3			.14			.02
4	.08[b]	.22	−.07[b]			.12
5				.34		.11
6	.32			.31		.20
7		.30		.39		.21
8			.14	.34		.14
9	.18	.13[b]	−.06[b]	.35		.22
			56 Districts			
10	−.22[b]					.05
11		.37				.14
12			.11[b]			.01
13	−.35	.44	.01[b]			.26
14				.52		.27
15	.16[b]			.50		.29
16		.48		.59		.44
17			.14[b]	.52		.28
18	.04[b]	.44	.01[b]	.51		.44
19					.49	.24
20	−.29				.52	.30
21		.35			.47	.33
22			.11[b]		.49	.25
23				.48	.44	.41
24	.04[b]			.40	.42	.41
25		.45		.55	.42	.53
26			.13[b]	.48	.44	.42
27	−.07[b]	.44	.02[b]	.40	.42	.54

[a] Partialed on all other independent variables in the equation.
[b] insignificant at 95 percent confidence interval.

ures of program input are used together they explain 41 percent of the variance. The three socioeconomic variables add relatively little explanatory power to the regression. The most important of them is urbanization. Literacy and per capita income are insignificant when they are included in the same equation with the two measures of program input and with urbanization.

Most of the variation which is statistically "explained" is explained by the variables measuring the program inputs into the district. The socioeconomic variables do have an effect, but they explain a much smaller proportion of the variance. It is plausible to assume that a better measure of program input could explain much of the residual variation in acceptance rates among districts. Such variables might include more refined measures of the quantity of program inputs and some measures of the quality of such inputs (e.g.,

TABLE V-4

CORRELATIONS (r's) AMONG VARIABLES
USED IN DISTRICT ANALYSIS

	246 Districts					
1. Acceptors/Population	1					
2. Percent Literate	.26	1				
3. Percent Urban	.33	.65	1			
4. Per Capita Income	.14	.47	.57	1		
5. Clinics/Population	.34	−.12	.15	.02	1	
	1	2	3	4	5	
	56 Districts					
1. Acceptors/Population	1					
2. Percent Literate	−.22	1				
3. Percent Urban	.37	.25	1			
4. Per Capita Income	.11	−.06	.26	1		
5. Clinics/Population	.52	−.64	−.07	−.02	1	
6. Workers/Population	.49	.06	.15	.03	.23	1
	1	2	3	4	5	6

the effectiveness with which the program is administered in a district or the length of training of extension workers).

It is useful to ask the question as to what would be the increase in the acceptance of family planning if some of the variables discussed above (particularly the program input variables) were allowed to vary. In Table V-5, the regression coefficients have been recalculated as elasticities to show the response that could be expected from a variation in a particular independent variable. The elasticity is independent of the units of measure involved. It can be interpreted to show the percentage increase in the dependent variable that would be associated with a 1 percent increase in the independent variable, all other variables remaining constant. Thus an elasticity of 0.39 for the extension worker/population ratio in equation 27 means that if the extension worker/population ratio is increased by 1 percent the ratio of family planning acceptances to population will increase by 0.39 percent. The elasticities have been calculated at the means of the variables in the specific equations and therefore have strongest relevance to "average" districts. The relevant conclusion that one might draw from this table is that more inputs would indeed lead to greater acceptance of family planning. If the relationships implied in the equations are stable, then we can expect a favorable response to a larger family planning program. It is not necessary to wait for urbanization or a rise in per capita income.

The statistical relationships do not tell us, however, whether the gains from such increases in inputs would be larger than the gains that might be generated by better organization or a different approach to the problem. Nor does the statistical analysis tell us what will happen if the relationships which we have discussed are not stable. If, for example, there is a progressive disillusionment with the program, then an increase in the overall magnitude of program inputs may do little other than offset the general decline in acceptance.

TABLE V-5

THE RESPONSE OF FAMILY PLANNING ACCEPTANCE TO VARIATION IN THE INDEPENDENT VARIABLES (PARTIAL ELASTICITIES[a])

Equation Number	Literacy	Urbanization	Per Capita Income	Clinics/ Population	Workers/ Population
			246 Districts		
1	1.04				
2		.63			
3			.70		
4	*	.59	*		
5				.36	
6	1.22			.40	
7		.54		.32	
8			.66	.36	
9	.89	*	*	.37	
			56 Districts		
10	*				
11		.54			
12			*		
13	—.56	.65	*		
14				.41	
15	*			.50	
16		.61		.43	
17			*	.41	
18	*	.58	*	.45	
19					.55
20	—.43				.57
21		.45			.50
22			*		.55
23				.33	.44
24	*			.36	.43
25		.52		.37	.37
26			*	.34	.44
27	*	.53	*	.33	.39

[a] Calculated at variable means from regressions with the program acceptance index as the dependent variable.

* variable insignificant at 95 percent confidence level.

The above analysis is thus largely consistent with the hypothesis that past variation in the number of family planning acceptors by district has been the result of variations in the inputs to the Family Planning Program. It is not at all consistent with the conflicting hypothesis that family planning acceptance is the result of the prevailing differences in the socioeconomic conditions in the districts. The implication is that if the situation prevailing in 1966 continues, the more inputs to the Family Planning Program, the greater will be the output.

SUMMARY OF THE ARGUMENT

It is useful at this point to summarize the argument of this chapter. We assumed in earlier chapters that acceptors of the IUD and sterilization would not have used any alternative methods of contraception in the absence of the Program. The assumption has been defended on three grounds. First, the general prevailing social and economic conditions are not yet favorable for a fertility decline in India. Second, available data concerning the characteristics of individual acceptors of government family planning services indicate that acceptors are selected for high parity, contact with program extension personnel and very little else. There is little tendency for the kind of selection along class and educational lines that we would expect if acceptors were the vanguard of an autonomous social movement towards fertility control. In other words, the data do not seem to indicate that the acceptors of government family planning services are shifting from alternative means of preventing births. Finally, at the district level the relatively low association between acceptance rates and various measures of social and economic development and the high levels of association between program inputs and outputs, indicate that the family planning program may very well have been the critical factor in determining acceptance.

There is one important difficulty with the entire argument. Our discussion has all been directed toward showing that the use of the IUD and sterilization is the result of the Program and is not part of a general movement that would have existed even without the Program. There still remains the possibility that some of the acceptors may be substituting these methods for some traditional methods of birth prevention. We know that fertility in India is not at the biological maximum, which implies that methods such as abstinence, coitus interruptus, or abortion are being used. Some couples may find modern forms of birth prevention preferable to the older ones. The data for determining the extent of such substitution are lacking, but our subjective feeling is that it is not very large—probably not in excess of, say, 20 percent. Our conclusion, then, is that we are justified in attributing most of the benefits of birth prevention to government investments in family planning.

To the extent that some of the users of the IUD or sterilization may be substituting for traditional methods or may, indeed, be influenced by the forces of change that we have discussed in this chapter, we feel that their numbers are probably more than offset by the conservative assumptions of the earlier chapters. In estimating the value of preventing a birth, we did not take into account second-generation effects, and our time horizon was only twenty-five years. In the analysis of the number of births prevented by the IUD or sterilization, we have used relatively old age distributions. Finally, and most important, we have restricted the analysis to the clinical methods for which good data are available. All of these assumptions work to understate the contribution of the Program. The implication is, then, that the benefits ascribed to the Program in Table IV-5 are as good an estimate as the inherent complexity of the situation will allow.

In order to derive and to defend our estimate of the economic impact of the Indian Family Planning Program, we have been obliged to make many assumptions. Given the poor quality of the data and the relatively weak empirical foundations of much of the underlying theory, one should not attach too much significance to the specific numbers that are involved. They should, rather, be considered as the best estimate that can be made in a very uncertain world. Inevitably there are a great many subjective judgments that have become a part of the analysis. The resulting estimate of the economic impact is thus to some extent an amalgam of subjective judgment and poor data, and it is specious to attempt to convey a sense of false precision. The "true" value of the Program as measured by the per capita income criterion may be one-third higher or one-third lower than shown in Table IV-5. The important point is that the benefits are so large that even a considerable reduction leaves family planning as a very favorable area for investment.

Two fundamental conclusions can be drawn from the first five chapters. The first is optimistic. The Program has had some effect, and India is already enjoying the fruits of its decision to use scarce resources for birth prevention. But there is a second conclusion, more important than the first, for which the answer is not nearly so optimistic. Has the Program generated the maximum benefits possible under the prevailing conditions? We believe the answer is no, and the next two chapters will be devoted to a defense of this assertion. Basically, our proposition is that there have been important returns from the money invested so far in family planning, but that a great opportunity has been lost by not making the returns much larger than they have been to the present.

NOTES

1. Similarly, in analyzing the returns from the capital investment in a foundry, we attempt to isolate the marginal contribution of the investment by subtracting the cost of other factors which are considered given. See Chapter I, p 5..

2. There are many sources that discuss the demographic transition. George Stolnitz, "The Demographic Transition: From High to Low Birth Rates and Death Rates," in *Population: The Vital Revolution*, edited by Ronald Freedman (New York: Doubleday & Co., Inc., Anchor Books, 1964), pp. 30–46, contains a general description of the society-wide changes taking place. The chapter on fertility in *The Determinants and Consequences of Population Trends*, Population Studies, No. 17 (New York: Department of Social Affairs, Population Division, United Nations, 1953), pp. 71–97, discusses the decline of fertility in Europe and North America and the characteristics of the first users of contraception. The use of contraception as one response to changes in mortality and the economic environment is discussed in Kingsley Davis, "The Theory of Change and Response in Modern Demographic History," *Population Index*, 29 (October 1963), pp. 345–366. See also Gösta Carlsson, "The Decline of Fertility: Innovation or Adjustment Process," *Population Studies*, 20, No. 2 (November 1966), pp. 149–174.

3. Davis, "Theory of Change and Response," p. 362.

4. This pattern was by no means universal. For contrasting views see William Petersen, "The Demographic Transition in the Netherlands," *American Sociological Review*, 25, No. 3 (June 1966), pp. 334–347; or J. William Leasure, "Factors involved in the Decline of Fertility in Spain," *Demography*, 16, No. 3 (March 1963), pp. 271–285. Also Irene B. Taeuber, "Demographic Modernization: Continuities and Transitions," *Demography*, 3, No. 1 (1966), pp. 90–108.

5. Due to the lack of adequate vital statistics, birth and death rates are estimated by comparing successive census returns. Such procedures require that assumptions be made about infant mortality rates before the estimates can be derived. The official estimates tend to be optimistic. For example, the Planning Commission has suggested that the expectation of life at birth in 1966 was on the order of 50 years. Government of India, Planning Commission, *Fourth Five Year Plan: A Draft Outline* (New Delhi, 1966), p. 346. P. M. Visaria recently carefully reviewed the evidence and has concluded that a more likely figure for 1966 would be 46.2 years. "Mortality and Fertility in India, 1951–1961," *Milbank Memorial Fund Quarterly*, 47 (January 1969), pp. 91–116.

6. India is reasonably typical of underdeveloped countries in the rapidity of the decline in mortality. See Kingsley Davis, "The Amazing Decline of Mortality in Underdeveloped Areas," *American*

Economic Review, Papers and Proceedings, May 1956, pp. 305–318. See Eduardo E. Arriaga and Kingsley Davis, "The Pattern of Mortality Change in Latin America," *Demography*, 6, No. 3 (August 1969), pp. 223–242, for a discussion of the comparison between mortality decline in Latin America, Europe and India; and Eduardo E. Arriaga, *Mortality Decline and Its Demographic Effects in Latin America*, Population Monograph Series, No. 6 (Berkeley: Institute of International Studies, 1970), Part IV for a discussion of the consequences of the rapid fall in mortality for the fertility response in Latin America.

7. Myrdal, *Asian Drama*, p. 1671, suggests that the change suggested by these figures, taken from census reports, has been considerably overestimated because of changes in the definition of literacy. The numbers for literacy and urbanization are taken from Government of India, Registrar General, *Census of India, Paper No. 1 of 1962* (New Delhi, 1962), pp. 325–327.

8. See Daniel Thorner, "Long-Term Trends in Output in India," pp. 103–128, and Kingsley Davis, "Social and Demographic Aspects of Economic Development in India," pp. 263–315, both in *Economic Growth: Brazil, India, Japan*, edited by S. Kuznets, W. E. Moore, and J. Spengler (Durham, N.C.: Duke University Press, 1955).

9. This pessimistic view of the possibilities for an autonomous fertility decline is widely shared. See, for example, Coale and Hoover, *Population Growth and Economic Development*, pp. 56–60, and Myrdal, *Asian Drama*, pp. 1392 and 1524.

10. Freedman and Takeshita report similar findings for the people who accepted family planning services as a part of the Taichung program. Acceptors differed from non-acceptors by age and parity but not by social characteristics. See Freedman and Takeshita, *Family Planning in Taiwan*, p. 180.

11. Simmons, "The Investment in Family Planning," Part II.

12. R. A. Krishnan, "Report Regarding Follow-Up of 1000 Sterilized Fathers" (Madras, 1966), mimeographed.

13. Department of Statistics, University of Kerala, Evaluation Study II: A Study on "Effectively Sterilized Wives" (Trivandrum, 1966), mimeographed. The study does not mention what proportion of the cases were sterilized in government clinics. Other work done by the University of Kerala group indicates that high status groups report more knowledge and use of contraceptive means other than sterilization, but as they also report higher fertility is it not clear what are the implications of this response. The conclusion that the acceptors of sterilization in Kerala have tended to come from the

lower status groups is confirmed by the useful reports of the Demographic Research Centre, Bureau of Economics and Statistics, Trivandrum.

14. Dr. Mukta Sen and Dr. D. K. Sen, "Family Planning Practice of Couples of Reproductive Age Group in a Selected Locality in Calcutta—June, 1965," *Journal of Family Planning*, 14, No. 1 (Sept. 1967), pp. 13–24. T. Poffenberger reports somewhat similar results from Gujarat. The upper class in the village which he studied used private sources for tubal ligation. Those people who used government family planning services tended to come from all sections of the population.

15. See K. G. Krishna Murthy, *Research in Family Planning in India*, Sterling Publishers, (Delhi, 1968) in a review of the literature through 1965.

16. The pages of *Family Planning News* and *Journal of Family Welfare* are replete with examples, and there are many unpublished studies. A useful bibliography of studies dealing with sterilization is by K. K. Kapil, "A Bibliography of Sterilization Studies in India, 1952–1968," *Newsletter*, No. 26, Demographic Training and Research Center, Chembur, (October 1968) and a similar bibliography for the IUD in Ashash Bhende, "A Bibliography of IUCD Studies in India," *Newsletter*, No. 31, DTRC, Chembur (Jan., 1970).

17. Madya Pradesh and Assam. The exclusion of these states left 246 districts for which data was available. A further fifteen districts, largely in Jammu and Kashmir and Himachal Pradesh, have been eliminated because per capita income data was missing.

18. I collected this information personally from the state Family Planning Bureau.

19. Government of India, Registrar General, *Census of India, 1961 Census, Paper No. 1 of 1962, Final Population Totals* (New Delhi, 1962), Statistical Tables, pp. 330–353, and Tables of Union Territories and other areas, pp. 356–359.

20. *Ibid.*

21. National Council of Applied Economic Research, *Interdistrict and Inter-state Income Differentials, 1955–6*, Occasional Paper No. 6, New Delhi, 1963.

CHAPTER SIX

Future Investments in Birth Prevention and Alternative Approaches To The Familial Context of Reproductive Decisions

EARLIER CHAPTERS have been largely concerned with the return to past investments in family planning. In the present chapter and the one that follows, we examine some ways by which the acceptance of effective measures to limit family size could be increased. Since virtually all births taking place in India take place in the context of the family, any efforts to prevent births must concentrate on altering the decisions of the family unit. The purpose of this chapter, then, is to provide a classification of alternative ways of approaching the family unit and to say something concerning the likely success of each approach.

In a recent article, Judith Blake has indicated some major difficulties in what is now the conventional debate concerning population policy.[1] There are two extreme positions in the debate. Fertility declined in the developed countries as the level of per capita income increased. Reasoning by historical analogy, "the development school of thought" has argued that fertility will decrease automatically (i.e., independently of government action) when the rise in per capita income is sufficient to have changed social attitudes enough so that it seems advantageous to potential parents to limit their fertility. From this point of view, population policies will have little effect without a transformation in the economic structure of society. Thus, Kuznets writes, "Major and lasting changes in demographic trends are dependent on major and lasting changes in the system of long-term rewards that the social and economic structure bestows upon its members."[2] The implication of the development school of thought is that government policy can do little to accelerate the rate at which births are prevented. Family-formation decisions are based on motivations deeply rooted in the existing order and will not be changed without a restructuring of the entire society.

Opponents of the development approach argue that waiting for development to transform social institutions is a counsel of despair. They feel that a direct government policy will have an effect on the number of births taking place. Since, as they see it, couples already desire fewer children than they actually have, appropriately designed programs can help them to achieve a completed family size closer to the desired size. Supply people with the means, in the form of knowledge and equipment, and they will limit the size of their families.

FAMILY-SIZE DECISIONS OF PARENTS

Despite the recognized drawbacks to the approach, I have found it advantageous to think of parents' decisions concerning the number of children they will have in terms of a modified version of the microeconomic model of consumer behavior.[3] In the economist's model of consumer behavior, the consumer is thought to have a utility function which he uses to rank the desirability of alternative combinations of goods to be consumed. A market-determined set of relative prices is then introduced as a constraint upon his actions. The consumer desires to achieve the highest level of satisfaction consistent with the relative prices existing in the market. This he does by equating the marginal rate of substitution of any two commodities with the price ratio and exhausting his budget. It is perfectly valid to think of the family as following an analogous pattern of behavior in its decisions as to how many children to have. There are complications arising largely from the fact that there is no obvious market for children. On balance, however, it is our opinion that the approach may have more advantages than disadvantages. In essence, we are suggesting that parents will behave *as if* they were rational. We do not mean to suggest that every potential parent weighs the pros and cons of having each additional child. Rather, we believe we will get more useful insight and better predictions if we analyze parental behavior on the assumption that parents are, indeed, rational than if we assume them to be irrational. Thus, in the following discussion we try to work out the consequences of rational behavior for parents.

There are many motives for parents to have children. Among the most important on the positive side are the satisfactions obtained from the parental role, the social status that may be gained through raising children, the old age security that children may provide, and the wages that children may return to the family. On the negative side it costs money to raise children. The parents, especially the wife, may have their ability to work impaired in the process of raising a family. The existence of a large family and a small budget means both physical and psychological deprivation. The health of the mother is affected by childbearing. These motivations, both positive and negative, can be divided into two groups. On the one hand we have non-economic motives that are largely determined by the social setting in which the couple finds itself; an example of this kind of motive would be the satisfaction parents obtain from playing the role of parent. This and similar motives for childbearing will be considered part of the parents' basic value structure or utility function. On the other hand, there are motives such as the anticipated earnings of the family children which are more objective. This latter type of motive can be either positive or negative, and we will call the entire complex of motives of this type the "price" of having a child.

Each married couple has a set of values, a normative framework that is used to compare alternative states of the world. Using their value system as a measuring rod, they are able to rank all possible combinations of children and other desirable objectives. Children are considered desirable in and of themselves. In a sense, they can be thought of as consumption. They yield satisfaction directly.[4] Thus, the family places very high value on the ability to have children, but there are other objectives which it also considers to be important. For example, the family not only wants children; it wants well-educated and well-nourished children. The parents want adequate housing and food for themselves. These various objectives conflict. No family can satisfy all of its desires. What they can do is rank various combinations of the objectives and take the most satisfying combination consistent with the contraints on their actions.

The constraints on the consumer's actions are the prices of the goods he wishes to purchase and the size of his budget. What are the analogous restrictions on the behavior of the parent? Some potential parents are infecund or subfecund; for them childbearing decisions are determined in large measure by physiological circumstances. But the vast majority of parents can potentially at least exercise a considerable amount of control over family size. Their decisions may be influenced by economic conditions. Children have a price, or an opportunity cost, that is paid out over a number of years. There are the costs of the birth itself, food for the child, education, wedding expenses, and inefficiency resulting from excessively divided pieces of land. On the other hand, there are real positive returns in the form of wages or labor services, old-age security, and perhaps others. The negative costs of raising the child, minus the positive instrumental returns provided by the child, represents the net cost of a child in any given year.[5] The present value of this time stream of costs can be thought of as the price of having a child. The term "price" is used to emphasize the fact that decisions regarding fertility must relate to costs spread over a long period of time. In reducing these costs to a single number some assumptions must be made about the time component. This price varies from family to family, depending upon circumstances, and may even vary within the family from parity to parity. It does not matter whether the price is determined in a market; even this kind of nonmarket price is a factor which parents must consider in making their decisions.

Given that the elements which make up the price of a child can be both positive and negative, the composite index can be either positive or negative. On balance we would expect the price of children, as defined above, to be negative. That is to say the costs of raising a child in most situations far outweigh any economic advantages that children may bring their parents. This is especially so when one considers the long (and expensive) delay between childbirth and entry into the labor force.

What is the difference between the parents' value system and what we are calling the price of children? There is no hard and fast rule for deciding how to categorize the specific elements which go into the decision as to family size. If a particular consideration (for example, the social and religious significance attached to having a son or the onus placed on a woman who delivers after her own daughter has given birth) seems to be largely determined by the culture and has little relationship to the market value of goods, it falls into the non-economic category. On the other hand, if we are dealing with a component of the decision process that has a fairly reasonable financial equivalent (for example, the money costs associated with childbirth or the anticipated wages that a male child might share with his parents), then it is placed in the category of a price. In the analysis of conventional consumer goods the distinction is based largely on the criteria of the market. In the case of decisions relating to family size, there is no market involved. As a result our distinction between the price that the parents must pay in having a child and the parents' value system may be arbitrary in some cases. For example, one often cited motive for having children is that the parents may expect the children to provide old age security. If this old age security is the equivalent of an annuity scheme then it should be thought of as part of the net cost of child rearing. If on the other hand the parents think of themselves as gaining status through having children who will provide for them, then the old age security motive may logically fall in the category of motives for childbearing described by the parents' value structure.

The distinction is important because the complex of motives underlying the parents' value structure is rooted in culture and is presumably subject only to a relatively slow influence from the outside. The elements of the price motivation may be more easily subject to change.

The third factor helping to determine the "rational" parents' decision as to family size is their budget constraint: that is, the limit placed on family action by the sum total of resources available to it. In this case, resources would probably mean income, present and anticipated. Income is determined by the family's control over economic resources, e.g., land and labor. In a society where a large proportion of economic activity takes place without reference to the market, a broad interpretation of income is in order. Here we are thinking of income as the command which the family has over resources which could potentially be marketed.

Thus, three sets of factors operate to determine the number of children that will be chosen by a married couple in full control of their procreative ability. First, they have a set of tastes or values, essentially non-economic in origin, which allows them to compare the desirability of any two combinations of children and other desirable goods. This set of values is determined by the socialization process and by the individual characteristics of the parents in question. Second, there is a set of prices determined by forces beyond the control of the parents which defines the rate at which additional children can be exchanged for other opportunities. Finally, there is a limited amount of resources available to the parent. From the parents' point of view, the optimal situation is one in which they are able to reach the highest level of satisfaction consistent with their budget constraint. Alternatively, the parents are in a position of maximum satisfaction when the extra satisfaction which they receive from the last child exactly equals the satisfaction they could get from the best alternative use of their resources. Since the price is a measure of opportunity cost, parents would increase their family size until the marginal non-economic value of the last child exactly equals the price that is paid as a consequence of having the child. If they had fewer children than this optimal number, then they could always improve their satisfaction by having more. On the other hand, each child beyond the optimal number would cost them more than it was worth in terms of extra satisfaction.

From what has been said thus far, it should be clear that there are a number of ways in which a family planning program can influence the decisions of parents. It can, first of all, attempt to change the tastes of parents. This objective might be best achieved in the long run through the skillful use of the educational system. It might also be possible to influence the values of parents who have long since left the educational system. Such, in fact, is one of the goals of the extension program. A second approach to influencing family decisions is to alter the factors which help determine the price of children to their parents. Thus, the cost of education or housing might be increased. Alternatively, the rewards from not having children could be raised through some sort of direct incentive system of the kind proposed by Enke.[6] By altering the terms on which parents can trade childbearing for other objectives, these policies change the price of children.

The family unit, of course, cannot satisfy its needs regarding children instantaneously. Therefore, the family tends to be in a situation at low parities where the marginal non-economic value of an additional child is larger than the price that parents must pay for having that additional child. But as parity increases, the net advantage of an increase in family size becomes less and less pronounced and eventually disappears. That is, at some point the extra non-economic advantages of an additional child is equal to or less than the price of the marginal child. It is at this point that the rational parent in full control of the situation will cease to bear children and will use his resources for other purposes. There is always the possibility of course that the parity at which additional children become a losing proposition may be high enough that parents will lose the physiological ability to reproduce before they decide not to have more children. Furthermore, it is quite likely that the family size goals as determined in this manner are inconsistent with the goals of the national population policy.

This entire situation can be represented graphically. Assume that all other goods except children can be thought of as one commodity—call it money. Then, for the individual parent one can graph the marginal non-economic value of going from one parity to another, using money as the numeraire.[7] The marginal value of an additional child is very high at the low parities and decreases as the parity goes up. At some point it may even become zero. In Figure VI-1, the MNV (marginal non-economic value) curve represents the marginal value of an extra birth. At the point marked P, it is zero, and at parities higher than P it is negative.

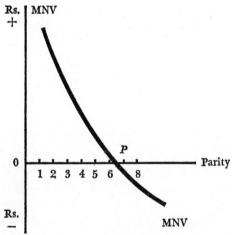

Figure VI-1. The Marginal Non-Economic Value of a Birth by Parity.

The price of an additional child may also, to some extent, be a function of parity. The labor services of the first child may be more valuable to the parents than those of later births, and old-age security may be more important for the first than for subsequent children. On the other hand, the first can pass on some things to the younger children, etc. Figure VI-2 shows price as a function of parity. It has been drawn as constant and positive for lack of knowledge of a more accurate representation.

The equilibrium number of children that will be chosen by a rational set of parents in full control of their ability to give birth to children will be where price and the mar-

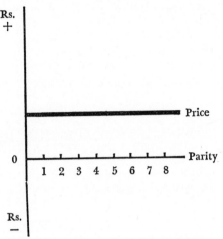

Figure VI-2. Price as a Function of Parity.

ginal non-economic value curves cross (Figure VI-3). Beyond the point designated as the equilibrium parity, the marginal non-economic value of an additional birth is lower than the price that has to be paid as a result of the birth. The equilibrium parity can be thought of as the dividing line between "wanted" and "unwanted" children, but it should be clear from the nature of the graph that the problem is not so much whether children are wanted, but how much they are wanted.

To this point we have been discussing the decisions of parents as to whether or not to have additional children. We have assumed that parents are in full control of their procreative potential. In the next paragraph, that assumption will be relaxed, but first it is useful to contrast the value of additional births as seen by the society with the parental view that we have been discussing.[8] In the last part of Chapter II it was concluded that the value of a birth prevented in India is positive and quite large; the welfare of the nation would increase if there were fewer births. That negative economic value of a marginal birth can be thought of as the

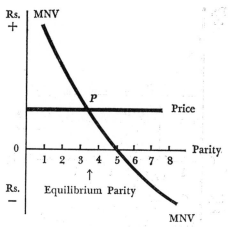

Figure VI-3. Equilibrium Parity for Parents in Full Control of Their Procreative Potential.

price that the nation pays for each additional birth. As it is superimposed on the graph in Figure VI-4, the implication is that the government should be willing to expend resources up to the amount shown by the value-of-a-prevented-birth line in order to prevent an additional birth.[9]

For the individual decision makers in the present underdeveloped countries, it is likely that the costs of having children will be lower and the benefits higher than they would be from the point of view of the Planning Commission, which represents the nation as a whole. The divergence results from the complex situation in which the parents find themselves. Some of the costs of raising children will be borne by society at large, by the extended family, or by the clan. Where there are costs for education, they are paid in large measure at public expense. Where the members of the joint family share the total product of their labor, the parents will not pay the full share of rearing the child. The benefits are also likely to be different than those seen by society. For example, the parent may consider the child as insurance for old age. Society, as a whole, does not need such insurance.

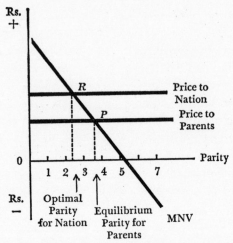

Figure VI-4. The Difference Between Optimal Average Parity for the Nation and the Equilibrium Parity for the Parents.

This divergence between the private and the social assessment of the value of a birth means that even a perfectly informed set of parents, completely in control of their reproductive potential, might place a higher value on marginal births than would the society as a whole.

In the above discussion we have analyzed parental behavior as if parents were rational and able to decide upon the number of children they desire. The implication of the discussion is that parents would go on having children until the extra satisfaction from a prospective additional child would be less than the price that would have to be paid. At this point we might consider the evidence as to the number of children that Indian parents seem to want. Surveys have indicated that the average Indian has a preference for a family consisting of about four children.[10] There are a number of ways in which this expression of preference can be explained. The most obvious interpretation would be that the average Indian couple wants to have four live births and, once having reached that parity, will place a zero or negative marginal valuation on any further births. But this interpretation is inconsistent with the observation that the average Indian couple that lives in unbroken marital union through the child-bearing period of life has between six and seven live births.[11] Are we to conclude that all of these extra births are unwanted? A second, more plausible interpretation of the ideal family size is that couples mean that they wanted to have at least four *living* children. Since mortality is still relatively high in India, many children die in the first years of life. Consequently, parents who wanted to have four children alive when they themselves were, say, fifty years of age, would certainly have to have more pregnancies in order to assure that they would achieve their goal.[12] If every child lived to maturity, then four live births would be sufficient to achieve the ideal family size, but under conditions of existing mortality, more are required. Exactly how many more is a difficult question which depends on the assumptions that are made about the parents' goals. It is probably fair to say, however, that parents would want at least one or two live births more, on the average, than the four necessary to reach the ideal family size in the absence of mortality.

In sum, then, there may be some discrepancy between desired family size and actual fertility performance, but it is not very large. Parents may now have, on the average, one or two more births than is consistent with the ideal family size they profess. How does the discrepancy arise? Why does the average family that survives through the reproductive period produce one or two "unwanted" births?

In our discussion of parental decisions we have assumed that parents were in full control of their fertility. To a large extent, such is not the case. The source of the problem is that sex has a utility to parents independent of the function it performs in permitting conceptions. Even when parents do not want any more children, they may still value sex highly enough to risk additional pregnancies. One could say that sex and children are jointly consumed sources of satisfaction—like bread and butter. In a society not fully informed concerning contraceptive techniques, the effect of the interaction is a vertical shift of the MNV curve (see Figure VI-5). The result is that even a rational parent may decide that sexual satisfaction more than offsets the risks of having a larger-than-ideal-number of children. Nor is the solution to the problem just a matter of introducing new knowledge to the community. The use of any contraceptive technique involves costs and uncertainties that may be quite substantial. In India, for example, many potential contraceptors seem to fear the possible adverse medical and social consequences of using the IUD or sterilization. Fear of medical complications alone may be one major reason why more couples are not using contraception. These concerns cause a shift in the MNV curve; in fact, the MNV curve may be shifted so much that it never reaches the price line. If this were the case, there would be no family size too large.

At an earlier point we discussed some of the implications for population policy of the simple model where parents are

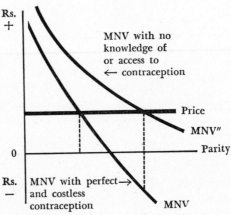

Figure VI-5. The Effect on the MNV Curve of Parents' Inadequate Control of Their Procreative Potential.

assumed to be in full control of their fertility. The complications of the last paragraph have further implications concerning the role of the Family Planning Program. One of
the important functions of the Program is to introduce
knowledge to the community that will permit the separation
of sex and procreation (Policy C). The Program can also
make devices available in such a manner as to minimize
the cost to the family of using contraception (Policy D).
But, as indicated in the discussion at the beginning of the
chapter, these activities are only two of the ways that the
government can attempt to influence the fertility behavior
of what we have termed "rational parents." The other two
approaches are to attempt to change the value structure of
parents—that is, to shift the utility functions in such a manner that fewer children are desired at any price (Policy A)
and to change the price of children in such a manner that
parents will find it less desirable to have more (Policy B).
Each of these four policies can be illustrated in terms of the
graphs shown earlier. Policy A (utility change) would involve shifting the MNV curve to the left as shown in Figure
VI-6. Policy B (price change) would involve shifting the price

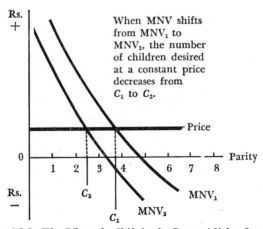

Figure VI-6. The Effect of a Shift in the Parents' Value Structure.

curve upward (Figure VI-7). Policy C (knowledge) would lead to a shift of the MNV' curve toward the MNV curve. The new curve, MNV'', would represent the simple MNV curve adjusted for the disutility of contraceptive use. Policy D (cost of contraception), which is very similar to Policy C, would involve shifting the MNV'' curve as close as possible to the MNV curve through the provision of supplies in the most convenient manner possible. A perfect contraceptive, provided in a perfect manner, would cause the MNV'' curve to be the same as the MNV curve. These last possibilities are shown in Figure VI-8.

Traditionally, population policy has placed greatest emphasis on Policies C and D. Such emphasis has led to the anomalous situation described by Davis, where adoptors are all of very high parity—such high parity, in fact, that even if the Program were fully successful in shifting the MNV' curve to the MNV curve, there would still be more births than the society can be expected to support.[13] If our earlier conclusion that there is relatively little discrepancy between

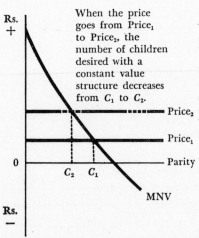

Figure VI-7. The Effect of a Rise in the Price Parents Pay for Children.

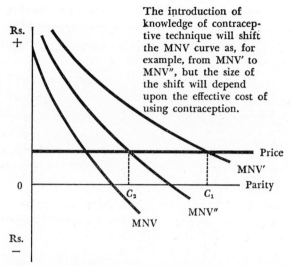

The introduction of knowledge of contraceptive technique will shift the MNV curve as, for example, from MNV' to MNV'', but the size of the shift will depend upon the effective cost of using contraception.

Figure VI-8. The Effect of Introducing Contraceptive Knowledge or Reducing the Cost of Contraceptive Use.

desired and actual family size is correct, then policies A and B may have potentially more impact since they are likely to affect women of lower parities. During the past few years the term "beyond family planning" has been used to describe the kind of policies which fall under the A and B classification which we are using here. The term "family planning" is thus reserved for policies classified under C and D.[14]

During the process of economic and social development, there will be a number of changes in the social structure that will affect the childbearing decisions of parents. It is, first of all, likely that tastes will change so that less value is attached to a large family size. Second, and perhaps most important, the price of children will probably rise. The value of their labor services does not increase, but the cost of education and the accepted standard of nourishment and shelter does. Finally, both increasing knowledge of contraception and the decreasing cost of using contraception which results from improved technology, work to favor increased success in limiting births. All of these changes took place in Western countries without the government being obliged to intervene, and it is likely that they would also take place in the presently underdeveloped countries as they manage to transform their economic and social structures. Needless to say, however, population growth is one of the major obstacles to the desired transformation of society. It is necessary, therefore, to seek alternative means of changing the parameters which affect the decisions we are discussing. The case for a population control program really rests, then, on the possibility of altering parents' decision-making framework without waiting until there has been a complete transformation of society in all spheres.

NOTES

1. Judith Blake, "Demographic Science and the Redirection of Population Policy." *Journal of Chronic Diseases,* 18 (1965), pp. 1181–1200.

2. Simon Kuznets, "Growth and Structure of National Product, Countries in the ECAFE Region, 1950–61," in United Nations, Economic Commission for Asia and the Far East, *Report of the Asian Population Conference and Selected Papers* (New York, 1964), p. 142. See, also, Frank W. Notestein, "Problems of Policy in Relation to Areas of Heavy Population Pressure," in *Population Theory and Policy,* eds. J. J. Spengler and O. D. Duncan (Glencoe, Ill.: Free Press, 1956), pp. 470–483; Davis' comments on the early view of Notestein in Davis, "Social and Demographic Aspects," p. 289; Simon Kuznets, "Population and Economic Growth," *Proceedings of the American Philosophical Society,* 111–113, June 1967, pp. 170–193; and Harry M. Raulet, "Family Planning and Population Control in Developing Countries," *Demography,* Vol. VII, No. 2, pp. 211–234.

3. See Gary Becker, "An Economic Analysis of Fertility" in Universities-National Bureau Committee for Economic Research, *Demographic and Economic Change in Developed Countries* (Princeton, N.J.: Princeton University Press, 1960), pp. 209–240. Becker's paper is critically reviewed by Judith Blake, "Are Babies Consumer Durables?" *Population Studies,* 22 (March 1968), pp. 5–25. I have also

found N. B. Ryder's discussion of reproductive institutions useful. "Fertility," in *The Study of Population: An Inventory and Appraisal*, P. M. Hauser and O. D. Duncan, eds. (Chicago: The University of Chicago Press, 1959), p. 426. Also Easterlin, "Towards a Socioeconomic Theory of Fertility;" Jacob Mincer, "Market Prices, Opportunity Costs, and Income Effects," in *Measurements in Economics: Studies in Mathematical Economics and Econometrics in Memory of Yehuda Grunfeld* (Stanford: Stanford University Press, 1963) pp. 67–82; Joseph J. Spengler, "Values and Fertility Analysis," *Demography*, 3, No. 1 (1966), pp. 109–130; Julian Simon, "The Effect of Income on Fertility," *Population Studies*, 23, No. 3 (Nov. 1969), pp. 327–341.

4. Some of the satisfactions Indian parents receive from their children are described in Morris E. Opler, "Cultural Context and Population Control Programs in Village India," in *Fact and Theory in Social Science* eds. E. W. Count and G. T. Bowles, (Syracuse, N.Y.: Syracuse University Press, 1964), pp. 201–221. See also Thomas Poffenberger, *Husband-Wife Communication and Motivational Aspects of Population Control in an Indian Village*, Central Family Planning Institute, New Delhi, Dec. 1969.

5. Harvey Leibenstein classifies the costs and utilities of children somewhat similarly in *Economic Backwardness and Economic Growth* (New York: John Wiley and Sons, Inc., 1963), p. 162.

6. Enke, "Government Payments to Limit Population."

7. The marginal non-economic value curve can be defined in a number of ways. One approach might be to have parents rank different combinations of children and other alternatives. Then with the known set of preferences and with the known budget constraint, the parity consistent with the highest attainable level of subjective well-being can be established. Moving away from this point of equilibrium, the marginal value of a birth can be established by asking how much compensation would have to be given to the parents to get them to change their family size from one parity to another. The cost of the compensation plus the original price represents the marginal non-economic value of a birth at the specific parity. The procedure can be repeated for each parity. Empirically the suggested procedure would be very difficult. The point is not to suggest a practicable procedure but to suggest some of the elements in the parents' decision making process. Basically the MNV represents the amount of compensation that would be required to adopt any given parity if the price of having children were zero.

8. Leibenstein, *Economic Backwardness,* p. 160. Also, see Kingsley Davis, "Population Policy: Will Current Programs Succeed?" *Science,* 158 (November 10, 1967), p. 732. J. J. Spengler, "Population Problem: In Search of a Solution" *Science,* 166 (Dec. 5, 1969), pp. 1234–1238.

9. Julian Simon would differ on this point. See Simon, "The Value of Avoided Births to Underdeveloped Countries," *Population Studies,* 23, No. 1 (March, 1969), pp. 61–68. See also Paul Demeny, "The Economics of Population Control."

10. For a list of many of the surveys, See S. N. Agarwala, "Population Control in India: Progress and Prospects," in the symposium on population control published in *Law and Contemporary Problems* (Summer 1960).

11. See Agarwala, *Population,* p. 37.

12. See Ronald Freedman, "The Sociology of Human Fertility: A Trend Report and Bibliography," *Current Sociology,* 10/11 (1961), p. 47. Heer and Smith have calculated the fertility required to give parents confidence that a son would survive until the father is sixty-five years old. Their results and the literature they cite support the notion that parents will adjust their fertility to obtain a desired number of living children. See David M. Heer and Dean O. Smith, "Mortality Level, Desired Family Size, and Population Increase," *Demography,* 5, No. 1 (1968), pp. 104–121.

13. Davis, "Population Policy," p. 735.

14. See Bernard Berelson, "Beyond Family Planning," *Studies in Family Planning,* 38 (Feb. 1969), pp. 1–16.

CHAPTER SEVEN

Constraints Inhibiting Expansion of the Program

THE ECONOMIC OBJECTIVE of the Family Planning Program is to maximize the social benefit accruing to the nation from its activities. This objective implies that the Program should be expanded until the marginal social return is exactly equal to the marginal social cost of the last birth prevented. Alternative estimates of the marginal social benefit are shown in the figures in Table II-2. The marginal social cost of a birth prevented is lower than the marginal social benefit by almost any measure. Consequently, it is important to examine the nature of some of the constraints that are preventing the expansion of the birth prevention program. We will argue in this chapter that it is possible to increase output of the present Program through the use of additional inputs or through the introduction of new procedures.

A brief re-examination of the recent history of the Family Planning Program sheds some light on the major problems. As indicated in Chapter IV, the number of new acceptors expanded every year through 1967–68 but has been decreasing during the past two years. There is no way of avoiding the conclusion that the momentum of the earlier years has been lost. The reasons for this state of affairs are not entirely clear. The bulk of this chapter will examine some of the problems that this outsider sees. But first it may be well to dispose of some reasons that do not explain the decline.

First, the problem of an appropriate technique does not seem to be the major limitation. The IUD has been relatively well received in countries such as Taiwan and Korea, and there is nothing unique in the Indian situation that would make the device less appropriate there than in those other countries. Sterilization is also an adequate means of birth prevention in the Indian context. Millions of men and women have been willing to use it in the past, and there is no reason to think that inherent defects in the method are causing the decrease in its popularity. In sum, new and improved techniques of contraception might benefit some potential users and might even increase the total number of users considerably, but there is no reason to assume that the lack of an adequate contraceptive is causing the decline in family planning acceptance.

Nor can we attribute the decline to the "skimming of the cream" theory which holds that the most highly motivated couples volunteered early in the program and as a result potential acceptors are increasingly difficult to recruit. Such a theory is inconsistent with the characteristics of the people who have been accepting the IUD and sterilization during past years and with the wide variability in acceptance rates by geographical region.

The large variation in rates of family planning acceptance by district was shown in Table V-1. Table VII-1 presents certain information concerning family planning performance by state and a number of characteristics of the populations living in the states. It is clear that there is a large variation in the rates of family planning acceptance, whether they are measured as a cumulative proportion or as a proportion of the population of the state accepting in 1968–69. The

TABLE VII-1
DATA RELATING TO FAMILY PLANNING BY STATE—
CUMULATIVE PERFORMANCE AND THE SITUATION IN 1969

State or Territory	1 Population ('000) est. 69-70	2 Sterilizations through Mar. '69	3 IUD Insertions through Mar. '69	4 Total IUDs and Steril. through Mar. '69	5 No. of IUDs and Steril. per 1000 pop.	6 % of Females Literate 1961	7 % of Pop. Urban 1961	8 68–69 FP Expend/ 1000 pop. (rupees)	9 % Required Tech. Staff in Position Dec. '69	10 Functioning Health Centers/ mil. pop.
Andhra Pradesh	42,647	478,780	183,585	612,365	14.36 (13)[b]	12.0	17.4	567	91	14.4
Assam	15,321	43,912	112,400	156,312	10.20 (15)	16.0	7.7	180	46	8.3
Bihar	56,787	308,392	102,091	410,483	7.23 (18)	6.9	8.4	267	65	11.9
Gujarat	26,069	332,405	156,332	488,727	18.75 (9)	19.1	25.8	669	56	13.4
Haryana	9,871	46,560	142,147	188,707	19.12 (6)	N.A.	N.A.	662	68	12.6
Jammu & Kashmir	4,008	32,409	33,046	65,455	16.33 (11)	4.3	16.7	730	20	18.5
Kerala	20,945	294,421	150,092	444,513	21.22 (5)	38.9	15.1	776	85	9.4
Madhya Pradesh	40,055	484,048	125,261	609,309	15.21 (12)	6.7	14.3	440	59	13.0
Madras (Tamil Nadu)	39,034	781,608	49,329	830,937	21.29 (4)	18.2	26.7	334	64	9.9
Maharashtra	49,210	931,644	311,273	1,242,917	25.26 (2)	16.8	28.2	484	56	12.2
Mysore	28,839	323,647	224,174	547,821	19.00 (7)	14.2	22.3	530	53	11.0
Orissa	21,283	307,091	93,471	400,562	18.82 (8)	8.6	6.3	546	73	17.1
Punjab	14,479	176,385	391,838	568,223	39.24 (1)	14.1	20.1	677	74	15.7
Rajasthan	25,771	126,931	73,911	200,842	7.79 (17)	5.8	16.3	524	56	11.7
Uttar Pradesh	89,425	549,390	345,654	895,044	10.01 (16)	7.0	12.9	400	50	10.6
West Bengal	44,074	471,915	281,115	753,030	17.09 (10)	17.0	24.5	508	66	8.1
Delhi	4,090	43,855	45,921	89,776	21.95 (3)	42.5	88.7	N.A.	N.A.	17.1
Himachal Pradesh	3,551	20,280	25,419	45,699	12.87 (14)	6.2	4.7	N.A.	N.A.	26.2
All India[a]	540,313	5,879,011	2,869,616	8,748,627	16.19	12.9	18.0	685	58	12.4

[a] Not a total, since some territories were omitted from this table.
[b] Rank order number.

TABLE VII-1 (Cont.)

MEASURES OF SUCCESS—1968–69 DATA

State or Territory	11 Population ('000) '69-70	12 Sterilization '68–69	13 Insertions '68–69	14 # of eligible couples ('000)	15 # of Ster. and Ins. per 1000 pop.	16 Present Value per capita of '68–69 Program (Rupees)	17 # of Ster. and Ins. per 1000 eligible couples	18 Present Value per eligible couple of '68–69 Program (Rupees)
Andhra Pradesh	42,647	203,821	17,048	4,423	5.18 (3)	56.6 (2)	49.9 (5)	545 (3)
Assam	15,321	14,731	21,791	1,313	2.38 (16)	15.7 (18)	27.8 (15)	183 (17)
Bihar	56,787	84,716	21,657	6,050	1.87 (18)	18.5 (17)	17.6 (18)	173 (18)
Gujarat	26,069	100,559	12,422	2,547	4.33 (9)	46.2 (4)	44.4 (9)	473 (5)
Haryana	9,871	19,347	29,464	881	4.94 (6)	32.4 (13)	55.4 (4)	363 (12)
Jammu & Kashmir	4,008	11,841	7,522	417	4.84 (7)	40.2 (8)	46.5 (8)	387 (10)
Kerala	20,945	73,840	36,062	1,696	5.25 (2)	46.3 (3)	64.8 (1)	573 (2)
Madhya Pradesh	40,055	134,357	35,524	4,295	4.24 (11)	41.7 (7)	39.6 (13)	388 (9)
Madras (Tamil Nadu)	39,034	116,955	23,812	3,866	3.61 (14)	36.6 (11)	36.4 (14)	370 (11)
Maharashtra	49,210	273,034	11,105	4,981	5.77 (1)	64.9 (1)	57.0 (3)	641 (1)
Mysore	28,839	92,256	19,717	2,746	3.88 (12)	39.2 (9)	40.8 (12)	412 (8)
Orissa	21,283	70,839	35,860	2,238	5.01 (5)	43.9 (6)	47.7 (6)	418 (7)
Punjab	14,479	38,676	36,248	1,290	5.17 (4)	39.0 (10)	58.1 (2)	438 (6)
Rajasthan	25,771	87,830	21,060	2,675	2.28 (17)	19.6 (16)	22.0 (17)	189 (16)
Uttar Pradesh	89,425	155,883	90,792	9,326	2.76 (15)	23.4 (15)	26.5 (16)	225 (15)
West Bengal	44,074	168,545	21,486	4,051	4.31 (10)	45.7 (5)	46.9 (7)	498 (4)
Delhi	4,090	8,865	6,704	365	3.81 (13)	30.3 (14)	42.7 (10)	340 (13)
Himachal Pradesh	3,551	7,936	7,704	370	4.40 (8)	32.8 (12)	42.3 (11)	316 (14)
All India	540,313	1,649,469	472,788	53,993	3.93	38.1	39.3	381

TABLE VII-1 (Cont.)

Sources and definitions:

1. India; Ministry of Health, Family Planning, Works, Housing and Urban Development; Department of Family Planning; "Monthly Statements on the Progress of Family Planning Programme in India," Statement I, New Delhi, February 10, 1970.

2., 3. *Family Planning News* 8 (August 1967), pp. 19–23; 9 (August 1968), pp. 20–23; 10 (August 1969), pp. 16–17.

6., 7. *Census of India*, Paper No. 1 of 1962, New Delhi.

8. Calculated from 1968–69 revised allocations in Statement Showing Expenditure on Family Planning Programme in Different States and Union Territories, in "Progress in Family Planning Program in India," Government of India, Ministry of Health, Family Planning and Urban Development, Department of Family Planning, November 1968, n.p.

9. "Monthly Statements of Progress," Statement VII. Percentage was calculated. Most data complete to December 1969.

10. "Monthly Statements of Progress," Statement IV and V. Sum of urban and rural health centers divided by population estimate 69–70.

11. "Monthly Statements of Progress"

12., 13. *Family Planning News*

14. "Monthly Statements in Progress." The number of *Eligible Couples* is arrived at by multiplying the number of married women in ages 15–44 in 1968–69 by 5/9, which has been taken as a practical approximation for the proportion sterile, pregnant and not practicing family planning due to ill health or desire to have a child, which factors render the women ineligible for adopting family planning method.

16. The present value of an insertion and of a sterilization are defined in Chapter IV.

Present value of benefits generated by the program in 1968–69 = present value of 1968–69 sterilizations + present value of 1968–69 IUD insertions. Present value per capita of 1968–69 Program = present value of benefits generated by 1968–69 program/population in 1969–70.

levels of acceptance in states such as Maharashtra and the Punjab have been nearly three times as high as the level in low performing states such as Bihar and Uttar Pradesh. Variation of this order is hard to reconcile with the "skimming of the cream" theory of program stagnation.

There are some important points about the state data that should be raised in passing. In the tables we have presented a number of alternative measures of program performance.

It is trivial to observe that expenditure on family planning is designed to achieve the goals of the program administration. But an examination of alternative measures of program performance can also be used to indicate what program administrators view to be their major goals. In this respect it is interesting that the measures of performance relating the absolute number of acceptors to the base population (as shown in columns 5 and 15) are more highly correlated with expenditure than are measures which relate the present number of births prevented to the population. The basic reason for this discrepancy is the differing emphasis on sterilization and the IUD in the various states. One possible interpretation of the data is that program administrators take as their goal raising the absolute number of acceptors and are much less concerned with the problem of preventing births.

It is often hypothesized that the inadequacies of the Indian Family Planning Program can be attributed to the inadequate performance of the administrative apparatus. The variations in the state data give some support to this hypothesis, but before turning to the question of administration of the Program as it is presently conceived let us review the many suggestions that have been made for a major change of strategy.

POLICIES THAT CHANGE TASTES AND THE PRICE PARENTS PAY FOR CHILDREN— A FUNDAMENTAL ALTERATION IN THE APPROACH TO BIRTH PREVENTION

Over the long run, the most serious limitation of the present Program is the narrow view that the government takes of the policy options at its disposal. In terms of the discussion in Chapter VI, very little attention has been given to policy approaches A and B—that is, to policies designed to change parents' inherent taste for children (their family-size norms) or to raise the price that they pay for having additional children to something more closely approximating the price paid by society as a whole. The intensity of parents' desire for children is probably learned at a relatively young age; it is not easy to affect these tastes if attention is restricted largely to older couples. The formal educational system may be the most effective channel for reaching the young, but the Program should make a real effort to reach all people while they are still of school age or while they are in the first years of marriage. The present emphasis is on contacting couples with more than three children. In fact, until recently, sterilization was not even permitted for men with fewer than three children who, although fully cognizant of the implications of their action, wanted to be sterilized.

Equally little attention has been paid to the possibility of raising the price that parents pay for children.[2] Preference for government jobs or positions in the schools could be based on small family size, just as prior military service is a basis for preference in U.S. Civil Service procedures. Perhaps scholarships could be given, for example, to only one child in any family. Promotions in the government service could take into account the size of the employee's family. Such policies do not win acceptance easily. Even comparatively mild reforms like removing the tax advantages associated with a large family have been resisted, presumably on the grounds that the children would suffer. On the other hand, since only the better-off segment of the Indian population pays direct taxes, this special consideration would seem to be very relevant.

There are also other ways of raising the cost of childbearing. The system of incentive payments suggested by Enke would function effectively to raise the price of having children. By having an additional child, one foregoes the possibility of receiving the incentive payment. With regard to sterilization, it should certainly be possible to devise a system of payments to give to persons who volunteer for the operation. The payments could be based on the number of children already born and on the likelihood of there being more births. At present, such payments as are given are very low, relative to the return on birth prevention. If they were raised to five or ten times the present scale, the price consideration alone might encourage many couples who would otherwise never use sterilization.

Incentive payments could also be associated with other forms of contraception, but the administrative difficulties involved are much greater. In India and Pakistan, where small payments were made to the women who had the IUD inserted, there is considerable evidence that the system has been abused. Some women removed the device in order to have it reinserted for the incentive fee. Such cheating by no means proves that there is no merit in the system of such payments. It only indicates the need for designing the schemes carefully. Perhaps it is best to predicate the payments on demonstrated lapses of time during which no pregnancy occurs.

Recent writings in the area of client incentives have stressed different ways of rewarding women who go for relatively long periods of time without becoming pregnant. Thus Ridker[3] has suggested that such women should be rewarded with a bond, redeemable after a relatively long lapse, which would partially replace the old age support that the parents could otherwise have expected from their children. The central problem with this kind of scheme is verifying that the reward is given at least most of the time to couples who would indeed have had more children if the reward were not offered to them. Unless an effective screening device can be devised, a disproportionate number of the couples participating in the scheme are likely to be secondarily sterile or using contraception even in the absence of the incentive. Some cases of this kind can probably not be avoided, but large scale abuse would probably lead to a quick demise for the program.

THE PROVISION OF INFORMATION AND SERVICES—SOME MEANS OF EXPANDING THE PRESENT PROGAM WITHOUT A FUNDAMENTAL CHANGE IN APPROACH

While changes directed at affecting tastes and the price that parents pay for children are extremely important, they should not obscure some of the immediate difficulties of the Program. Even in terms of the limited approach used in the past, the Program's impact has been less than expected. In 1970, 18 years after its official announcement, and eight years after a major reorganization, the reduction in the birth rate was on the order of 10 percent at best. It should have been possible to accomplish more than has been done up to the present. What have been the bottlenecks?

In the following discussion we will direct our attention to two kinds of problems that have hindered the expansion of the Program. First, we will talk about difficulties that have been experienced in finding the human and material resources needed as inputs for the government's family planning activities. Second, we will address ourselves to the organizational problems that have made these inputs less effective than they might have been otherwise. Our discussion of the problems experienced in trying to expand Program output is, of course, incomplete. We are only trying to assess some of what seem to us the most important limitations on Program output. Even such difficulties as we do discuss are not given the attention they merit.

On the whole, the Indian Family Planning Program has been well organized, especially when the standard of comparison is taken to be other official efforts to institute social change, whether it be the Community Development Program in India or the Job Corps in the United States. The fact is that the effort to change the fertility behavior of the population probably places more strain on the administrative system than most other governmental activities. Objectives are difficult to define, and in any case do not receive strong public support. Success is not easy to recognize and the work that must be done to accomplish it is extremely difficult to administer. But these problems make it doubly important that efforts be made to define problems quickly and accurately.

SHORTAGE OF HUMAN AND MATERIAL RESOURCES

Probably the most important shortage faced by the presently constituted Family Planning Program is the lack of sufficient trained personnel at all levels.[4] In every state there are key jobs that remain unfilled due to the lack of qualified persons. The problem is particularly acute in some of the less developed states such as Rajasthan, where working conditions are hard and the pay is no better than it is in more developed areas. At the beginning of 1967, for example, Rajasthan had several hundred unfilled medical positions in the Family Planning Program.[5] The shortage of trained staff is not restricted to medical positions. There is also a great shortage of auxiliary nurse midwives and female health visitors, of extension educators and other skilled personnel. In Rajasthan in 1967, to continue the example, there were 1,109 vacancies in the 1,160 positions for auxiliary nurse midwife in the rural clinics. Rajasthan is a relatively backward state, but the situation with regard to personnel is by no means unique. Shortages of personnel exist in varying degrees in all of the states of the Indian Union. The problem is especially difficult with regard to certain positions. Every state has a shortage of woman doctors. Only 108 of the 680 positions for woman doctors attached to District Headquarters in the various states of India were filled in 1967—a particular handicap given the importance that was attached to the IUD program at the time. Moreover, the situation has not improved very rapidly. As of the beginning of 1970 there were only 218 of 657 positions filled.

This shortage of trained people is a very important bottleneck. Without the planned number of skilled family planning personnel, the Program cannot function as designed, and there can be no test of its inherent ability to prevent births. The crucial question, however, is not whether there are shortages, but whether the existing shortages are unavoidable—i.e., they could not have been anticipated and corrected at an early date and/or could not have been avoided through the substitution of other resources. Indications are that the shortage of trained personnel could have been avoided and, where it was impossible to avoid, substitution would have been feasible.

There is no basic shortage of trained manpower in India; in fact, many policy makers are worried about the phenomenon of educated unemployment. The problem is that people have been trained, in large measure, for the wrong skills. The Indian universities overproduce graduates in arts and commerce and underproduce professional specialists.[6] They do not turn out the required number of doctors, despite the fact that the targets have been exceeded in both the Second and Third Five Year Plans.[7] The difficulty is that the government has consistently underestimated the required number of doctors. As a consequence, the ratio of doctors to population has not changed very much and there are few additional doctors available for special duty on family planning. The shortage of doctors is compounded by a very poor geographical distribution. West Bengal has proportionately more doctors than most other states in India, and throughout the country it is more difficult to find doctors to work in the rural areas than in the cities.

The problems associated with securing an adequate number of technical and extension personnel such as auxiliary nurse midwives have been similar to those of training doctors. The major difference is that it is easier to train ANM's because their training period is shorter and the required staff for the training institutions are not as scarce as for medical training. Still, there is a very real shortage of women trained as ANM's. The shortage has come about through the insufficient recognition of the manpower requirements associated with the expansion of the Family Planning Program.[8] The point that needs to be stressed in this discussion is that if the Program had been accorded the priority which the Plan's documents would have led one to expect,[9] then the same efforts that are being made today could have been made earlier, and the shortage of medical and para-medical personnel would not be so pressing.

We have argued in the above paragraphs that it would have been possible, with a reasonable amount of foresight, to anticipate the needs of the Family Planning Program in terms of trained personnel, but if we assume for a moment that the manpower goals of the Program were impossible, then there is the question of *equivalent substitutes* for the missing services of the untrained medical and para-medical staff. Doctors are especially trained to diagnose medical problems and to provide medical services. To what extent do the doctors employed by the Family Planning Program actually use their medical training? Doctors are involved, to a very large extent, in the administration of the Program. Such involvement is not always useful to the Program. Certainly, administrative skills are not easily learned in medical school. Moreover, many of the medical skills required for the Family Planning Program are of a repetitive, relatively uncomplicated nature that could be performed by para-medical personnel with adequate special training. The insertion of the IUD is a crucial case in point. The shortage of woman doctors is, to a very large extent, the result of their required use for IUD insertions. Experiments have been conducted in a number of countries and in some parts of India,[10] permitting para-medical staff to do IUD insertions. Two lessons have come out of that experience. The first is that under some conditions the para-medical staff can handle the routine problems associated with the IUD just as well as women doctors. The second is that they must be carefully trained, under strict supervision, in correct insertion procedures—this training to include actual IUD insertions by the trainee. They should also be able to refer difficult cases to fully qualified doctors.[11] Very little progress has been made in implementing full scale use of para-medicals when doctors are not available.

There are other types of substitution that have been tried and their use might be extended. Since there are not enough government doctors to carry the whole burden, private doctors are paid by the government at the rate of Rs. 30 per sterilization and Rs. 12 per IUD insertion for any family planning work they perform. IUD's inserted in the offices of private medical practitioners are just as effective in preventing pregnancies as are those inserted in government clinics. Presumably, if the price were high enough, private doctors would find it advantageous to take over many jobs now performed by government doctors. A start has already been made in this direction.[12]

A second area where substitution is possible is in the extension program. The job of the extension worker is to inform people of the existence of contraception and to convince them to use it. The job is not unlike that of a salesman. The canvasser program in Madras has already demonstrated that the use of private agents, paid by the number of cases they bring to the government hospitals, works and is cheaper than the extension programs in developed states such as Maharashtra.[13] If extension workers are hard to recruit and train, then they could be replaced by relatively untrained private individuals. Of course, in the process of substituting private for public channels, it is important to exercise some caution. The Madras Program requires that any man to be vasectomized must fall within certain age groups and that he have at least three children and the written permission of his wife. Any or all of these conditions have been violated on occasion by "canvassers." On the other hand, there is good evidence that canvassers show at least as much, if not more, solicitude for the welfare of the individual case. They do so because the cases recruited by the canvasser are employed by him to find more cases. Thus there is a very direct interest on his part in the well-being of the cases he finds.

Shortages of *material inputs* have not handicapped the Program nearly as much as the scarcity of trained family planning personnel. Nevertheless, greater expenditures on some of the inputs might have helped to raise the output of the program. Perhaps the most important input that has been lacking is transportation and communication facilities that make the jobs of the extension workers and doctors easier. The most obvious shortage has been that of vehicles. Doctors and their staffs need cars or jeeps to reach the remote rural areas. Other forms of transportation, such as walking or bicycles, take so much time and energy that these people spend more time on the road than they do in exercising their professional skills. Unfortunately, in 1967 many of the rural Primary Health Centers did not have vehicles and only a few had more than one.[14] Associated with this problem of transportation is the related problem of communications. It is not unusual for the medical staff of the district headquarters to undertake the difficult trip to some remote village only to discover that the cases they had been assured would be present could not be located, or for the extension workers to prepare cases only to have the medical staff fail to appear at the appointed time and station. Such difficulties might easily justify relatively large expenditures on improved telephone communications with the remote Primary Health Centers and Subcenters.

The question of expensive material resources is central to the problems of resource allocation for development. There is some evidence, however, that the Family Planning Program has been neglected because of the fact that its needs are not so clearly of a material kind as are those of an industrial establishment. A great deal of concern has been expressed over the use of foreign exchange to finance imports of vehicles or even contraceptive supplies. Because of decisions to conserve on foreign exchange, apparently there was a shortage of condoms during much of 1966, and one of the grounds for not making more use of oral contraceptives has been their high foreign exchange cost. It is important to remember that to make an equivalent contribution to economic development as that which is made by preventing a single birth, an amount of foreign exchange will be required far in excess of that which would be used in the Family Planning Program. Thus, efforts to conserve foreign exchange by not buying Program inputs outside of India are penny-wise and pound-foolish.

One important point brought out by the input shortages for the Family Planning Program, and also by the discussion of alternative approaches to the family, is that the Program is in no way an isolate. It is absolutely necessary that it be considered an integral part of the national effort of social and economic development. For example, investments in education will have an impact on the Program in two ways. First, they will increase the pool from which the skilled workers needed for the Program can be drawn and, second, education makes the general population more responsive to family planning. Thus, investments in education are not at all independent of investments in family planning and, ideally, with enough information, we would be able to deal explicitily with some of the interdependencies. A second example is that of the needed scarce inputs for family planning. The use of both domestically produced inputs and inputs that must be purchased from abroad means that there will be fewer resources available for alternative investments. Thus, on all counts it is important that, for optimal investment allocation, strong efforts be made to consider the Family Planning Program a regular part of the national development effort.

In the preceding pages we have argued that the shortages that have handicapped the Program should have been anticipated and corrected, and that even without correction it would have been possible to find substitutes for many of the missing skills. There is one other related but important problem that demands attention. This is the type and quality of the organization which directs the Family Planning Program. In this area there are two distinct problems. The first is in the organization of the Program to implement the policies that have been chosen. The second is the organization that makes the original suggestions for policy. Most of the remaining discussion in this chapter will be directed to the former problem.

ADMINISTRATIVE PROBLEMS IN THE STATES

Because health (and, therefore, family planning as conceived by its organizers and proponents) is a subject where the individual states of the Indian Union have precedence, there is considerable variation in the administration of the Family Planning Program. The program of birth prevention in India has had its greatest success in those states where the level of administration, both in health and in the area of unrelated government activity, is generally considered to be high, and it has been relatively unsuccessful in those states where administration is considered poor. Thus, in Maharashtra, where the level of administration has been high, the Program has performed well. In Haryana, where the administration is good, but the population is considered "backward," the response to the Program has been impressive. In the States of Bihar and the Uttar Pradesh, where the level of administration is low, Program performance has also been poor. The important role of organization inputs as an independent determinant of family planning acceptance at the district level has already been discussed in Chapter V.

The key to good administration seems to lie in the creation of an organization where the individuals concerned have a firm idea of their roles in the organization, feel those roles to be important, and are given the means to carry them out. The performance of individuals within the system is thus very much dependent upon the characteristics of the organization as a whole. In the following discussion, we try to isolate some of the organizational problems inherent in the implementation of the Program.

Many of the problems of the family planning organizations seem to relate to the role of doctors. Doctors are expected to provide much of the leadership at the block and district levels. The general shortage of doctors was discussed earlier. It is important to note, however, that even when doctors are in position, there are immense pressures operating to divert their attention from family planning to other responsibilities. In India family planning is integrated at all levels with the general health services—both curative and preventative. Moreover, these pressures have increased as the staff and responsibilities of the Primary Health Centers have increased. Often the Family Planning Program shares personnel and facilities with other health programs. For example, in most of the states, there is a single Block Medical Officer responsible for all government, medical, and public health services. Family planning is just a small part of his overall responsibility. Moreover, at the level of the block, medical personnel function simultaneously in their technical capacities and as the general administrators for the Program.[15] When the Block Medical Officer is a man of exceptional capabilities, this arrangement is adequate, but in most cases where the man is of normal abilities, administration suffers. The extension workers are not given the leadership they require. When we interviewed twenty-two extension workers, their complaints consistently referred to the lack of coordination between their activities and those of others. They were especially distressed at the problems of coordinating their activities with those of the medical personnel.

In many respects it seems wasteful to employ doctors as the administrators of the Family Planning Program. Administration is not a specific skill of the medical profession and there is a great need for medical services in the stricter, curative sense. Ideally, it should be possible to find an arrangement which would permit part of the responsibilities of administering the Family Planning Program to be given to professional administrators. The desired consequence would be both a larger administrative input to the Program and the release of medical skills. The principle reason why such a partitioning of the leadership role in the Family Planning Program has been resisted is that doctors are understandably reluctant to see their professional autonomy challenged. Doctors within the United States have been similarly reluctant to let professional administrators run hospitals. If a means could be found to increase the input of non-medical administrative skills, the rewards would be considerable. As we have argued in Chapter IV, the returns to the Family Planning Program are very high, and the responsibilities of running a state family planning program, or even a district program, are at least as great as those associated with running a large industrial undertaking. Thus good administrators will not find their talents wasted in the Family Planning Program.

As the Program is presently conceived, the main link between the Program organization and the general population is the extension worker. Much of the success of the Program depends upon his performance. There is a very heavy workload implied in the job description for extension positions. The extension worker is expected to spend a good deal of his working time visiting the villages in the block for which he is responsible. In the villages he is supposed to contact individual families and community leaders to familiarize himself with special village problems. This type of work is not easy. The villages are often far from the block headquarters. Villagers are sometimes hostile and commonly indifferent. Moreover, most of the village residents are not of the same educational status or social background as the extension worker. A dynamic personality and great resourcefulness are required of one who would succeed in this job.

The extension worker is at the bottom of the administrative hierarchy. He is not very well paid, but the job has all the desirable security characteristics of service with the Indian government. The one case which I encountered of a determined effort to remove an inadequate extension worker from her job required eighteen months and a number of special appeals before it was successful. Usually the medical officer in charges does not even bother. The work of an extension worker is very difficult to supervise, since much of it involves visits to the villages. Moreover, for the reasons discussed above, the block medical officer has little time for supervising the extension worker and there is little special reward for good performance. Most of the jobs are so defined that it is hard for a worker to be promoted from one level to another—even upon demonstrated competence. For example, the Block Extension Educator is expected to be a matriculate and the District Extension Educator must be a M.A.[16] Thus, persons who perform well in the lower-level job have little hope of being promoted. Nor is there any financial incentive for doing extra hard work. The main advantage of the position is that it is a secure job in a society where employment is scarce. It is little wonder, then, that persons employed in these positions do not always perform at their best. Among the districts of Maharashtra—a state with a very good record—the ratio of IUD insertions or sterilizations to extension personnel was about four per person, per month, during 1966–1967. Responses to some interview questions may make the viewpoint of the extension workers clearer.

When twenty-two extension workers, male and female, from three different North Indian states were asked whether they thought they would get any reward for doing their job especially well, twenty—almost all of them—replied that they would not. Most of them said their work was reviewed by their supervisor only once a week or once every two weeks. When they were asked if they thought they could perform better if they were given incentives for bringing in cases, many said they could. Many of these people were good performers from a relative point of view, but their responses give the picture of a locked-in group with little hope that job performance will improve their future employment opportunities.

The fault lies not so much with the individual workers as with the system. The bureaucratic structure of the public health service in India is similar to that of other government departments, such as community development or the general administrative services. Jobs are compartmentalized, underpaid with no marginal reward for marginal services rendered, and with no hope that negative incentives (i.e. threats) will have any effect. The jobs offer permanent security, but with no extra reward for extra effort. As a result, the average extension worker is reluctant to spend the full amount of required time in the field. He does not work particularly long or arduous hours, and the results of his labors reflect the lack of effort that is involved. An additional problem is that many of the extension workers employed in the Program have an urban or upper class background. As a result they often find it difficult to work among village and especially lower class populations.[17] These difficulties are particularly grievous in view of the data discussed in Chapter V, which indicate that the extension staff is a very important element in recruiting family planning adoptors.

There are ways of encouraging grass-roots initiative. A first general approach is to by-pass the system. It is interesting that the Family Planning Program has been a pioneer in breaking out of the old administrative patterns. We have already mentioned two possible innovations: the Madras canvasser system and the efforts to involve private medical practitioners in family planning. A third example is the use of private organizations to distribute contraceptive supplies and services. The government today is already using the medical services of some of the larger industrial and plantation companies to spread the use of family planning. It has also subcontracted much of the responsibility of distributing the government brand of condoms to a group of large private companies with extensive retail outlets. In all these approaches the government is relying on private contractors to carry out some part of the task of increasing the use of family planning. If the rewards are high enough, these programs will be at least as successful as the government equivalents.

A second approach is to restructure the administrative services. Incentives can be built into the system. Extension workers at any level, who do unusually well by some objective standard, can be advanced directly or can be sponsored for further training at training institutions or at the university to fit them for higher posts. Small financial rewards or bonuses can be given to those persons who do the best job. Such reforms have been considered, but the government has hesitated as it involves quite a radical change in organizational principle. A restructuring of the system would have strong implications for administrative services external to the Family Planning Program. A system of internal incentives for good performance in one area might lead to demands for change in others as well, and the Government of India cannot be expected to move rapidly in this area.

ADMINISTRATIVE PROBLEMS AT THE CENTER

Most of the previous discussion has concentrated on problems at the lower levels of Family Planning Program administration. These problems often have their source in the directives issued from the Center. There are fundamental problems of organization at the Center itself which make it difficult for the decisions to be as rapid and as well thought out as are required to give the Program real dynamism. We will comment here only on two problems—the inadequate feedback of information to the decision makers at the Center and the professional bias toward the health professions in the family planning bureaucracy.

Consider the responsibilities of the Center—that is, of the Department of Family Planning of the Ministry of Health, Family Planning, Works, Housing, and Urban Development. It is the responsibility of the Center to assess the fundamental problem of why there are so many births taking place, to suggest the most efficient way of reducing their number, to help the States organize the actual conduct of the birth-prevention campaign, and, finally, to reassess the Program in the light of ongoing experience. All of these responsibilities require the availability of large amounts of information.

To assess the fundamental problems associated with fertility control, much more basic demographic data is required than is presently available. Some of this information could be collected relatively easily. For example, the Registrar General's office and the National Sample Survey have both done useful work in estimating Indian fertility and mortality. It should be possible for these or other organizations to repeat such fact-gathering annually (and possibly to provide other information as well), and to finish the tabulations rapidly enough so that the results can be used immediately. Such efforts are expensive, but the money would be well invested. At a somewhat deeper level, there is still very little known concerning the determinants of demographic behavior in India. To what extent are the economic factors discussed in Chapter VI relevant to fertility? How does infant mortality affect fertility? How often does the average Indian couple have intercourse? What is the incidence and importance of abortion? What is the explanation for the relatively low marital fertility rates in the age groups over thirty? What is the role of abstinence?

The information available for the supervision of ongoing work is also very limited. Even the fundamental data concerning the number of IUD insertions and sterilizations do not seem to have been systematically checked. There is little information concerning the number and characteristics of couples using other contraceptive techniques. There is also a lack of information concerning the availability of inputs at the various States. For example, in the monthly progress reports there is no effort to estimate the number of extension workers in the field in each State. The fact that there are figures given for the number of peons working at the State government level indicates the somewhat erratic coverage of these statistics. It is difficult to assess the performance of different units if neither the basic number of inputs that are being used nor the quality of the statistics on output is known. The above kinds of information are essential for evaluating alternative ways of changing the Program. Since the Family Planning Program in India is decentralized in many respects, and since the State Programs vary themselves, detailed information concerning inputs and outputs would help the lagging States to benefit from the experience of the more successful States.

Policy makers also require information about the work practices of the people working in the organization. Everyone is aware of course of the work patterns that are supposed to exist, since they are published as a part of the job descriptions. But much less is known about the actual practices which prevail in the field. How many hours a day do the various categories of extension workers spend in the field or on record keeping? What proportion of the Block Medical Officer's time is spent on family planning as opposed to his other responsibilities? What different methods of approaching the target population are being employed by the extension staff and with what effect? What proportion of villages and/or couples have ever been approached by representatives of the Family Planning Program? To what extent does training improve the performance of the staff at different levels in the organization?

Other kinds of information are useful for purposes of Program evaluation. It took a long time for the Center to get any kind of feedback on the problems arising in connection with the IUD. Little hard data were available concerning the complications experienced by IUD users or the length of time that the IUD was retained by representative users. Such information is vital for the decisions involved in choosing the fundamental techniques that will be pushed by the Program. It is also vital for dealing with the operational consequences of adverse reactions to particular aspects of the Program. If there had been more complete and immediate feedback on the IUD, much could have been done to counteract the damaging spread of rumors concerning the device. The demise of the IUD program can be in large measure attributed to the informational vacuum in which the government was operating. It is not clear that recent handling of the Nirodh condom distribution program has been better. Little can be done in this area until the evaluation sections at the Center and in the States are enormously strengthened. At present less than one percent of all expenditure is estimated to go into evaluation.

The example of the IUD raises another important problem. There have been efforts to generate some of the data that we are discussing, but all too often they have been directed toward unrepresentative populations, i.e. urban hospital patients or the residents of rural areas that have had many times more inputs per resident than is possible in a representative operation. Thus, there were attempts to assess the retention of the IUD, but they were largely directed toward the urban populations. The urban studies often were well done, but they did not provide the basis for an adequate assessment of the Program. What was and is still needed is data which will permit generalization to the Program at large. A great deal of attention has been given to what are known as Action-Research Programs. Many of the Action-Research units have done good work in demonstrating that they can get the Indian population to respond to family planning programs, but in their pilot projects they have utilized more supervisory and/or extension staff than would be available under normal circumstances. At the same time, on-going State programs that have been unusually successful (Madras, Punjab, Maharashtra) have not been subjected to the kind of careful scrutiny that might give some clues as to how the Program should be run in other States.

One of the major results of the informational gap is that important decisions are made too late or not at all. This means that births are taking place that might have been prevented. Thus, the lack of information has a very high cost. The lack of sufficient information is the single largest problem for the decision makers at the Center. It is also a crucial problem at lower levels in the system. Greater attention to the gathering of information would yield a high payoff in terms of better decisions.

There is one additional problem concerning the process of making decisions at the Center which has to be discussed. The Family Planning Program has been considered all too long the sacred preserve of the medical and public health professions. While there is no doubt that these professions have a large contribution to make to the Program, their dominant role over the past years seems to have led to a comparative neglect of the Program by economic policy makers and politicians. As we have attempted to argue, the Family Planning Program is an integral part of the effort to transform the Indian economy, and there is every indication that the rate of return on additional expenditures in family planning is far greater than it is in any kind of industrial investment. It is probably fair to say that if economists and other social scientists devoted as much attention to different ways of preventing births as they do to other investments, substantial improvements would result. Much the same thing can be said concerning the political support that the Program receives. A good part of the reason for the neglect by economists and politicians is that they believe the Program falls within a technical area beyond their competance. "Leave it to the doctors" is the attitude, but there is much evidence that the doctors are not as expert as might be desired in such areas as public administration, communications, family sociology, economics, and many of the other fields that are as central to the problems of the Family Planning Program as is the physiology of sex.

Perhaps it is too vague to be useful, but there seems to be something to the "sociology of knowledge" problem in this case. Myrdal cautions us that we should search our professional motivations carefully to free ourselves of biases of various kinds.[18] It seems to me that in the area of family planning, important distortions are introduced into the way in which we attempt to apply knowledge to the difficult task of preventing births. There is, first of all, the prior claim of medicine to have discovered the problem before other professions. Then there is the devotion of professional economists to the traditional concerns of their profession—national finance, the allocation of investments within industry, and problems of pricing and the regulation of markets. There are so many fascinating problems involved in these areas that economists are willing to leave the field of family planning to the medical profession. The same might be said of the profession of public administration and management. How much more exciting it is to direct the operation of a public corporation than it is to be responsible for the operation of the Family Planning Program at the district level. Yet all indications are that the social contribution of the latter could be much more important than that of the former. On balance, there seem to be forces operating that give the Family Planning Program more orientation toward the health professions than would be optimal.[19]

PROSPECTS FOR THE
FUTURE EXPANSION OF THE PROGRAM

Many of the comments made in the last pages may seem unnecessarily harsh. The purpose is not to make useless criticism concerning the inadequacies of past administrative performance. Rather, it is to indicate the full range of possibilities for improvement. To solve a problem as complex as the one under consideration here, there is likely to be a wide range of possible solutions, each one of which will have associated with it different expectations for success. At the one extreme it would be possible to continue with the same patterns of reform used in the past—gradual, well considered, and safely within the existing system. On the other hand, it would be possible to pull all the stops and apply every resource and organizational tool available for finding a solution. We will not make any attempt to assess the exact future course likely to be taken by the Family Planning Program. There are some conclusions that should, however, be drawn from the discussion of the present and the preceding chapter.

Two major kinds of obstacles are operating to prevent the widespread adoption of family planning in India. First there are clear indications that most Indian parents find a relatively large number of children fully consistent with the over-all social objectives which they have set for themselves. When adjustment is made for mortality expectations, the desired family size is not very different from actual family size. Thus improvements in the way family planning information and services are made available is not likely to be very successful unless more is done to change the fundamental set of rewards that parents get from their children. That implies high incentive payments to parents, education for younger people before they are married and saddled with large families, and the introduction of any possible measures to make child-bearing an unattractive pattern of life. To get the birth rate to significantly lower levels, it may be necessary to follow the suggestions of Blake that the family structure itself should be undermined. All of this implies rather drastic changes in the way parents look at the world and it is not yet clear whether national leaders in India (or elsewhere) are sufficiently development minded to be willing to pay the price.

Despite this fundamental problem of motivation, there is vast room for improvement in the way in which the present Program is conducted. Under existing conditions people working at the lower echelons have relatively low morale and commitment, are poorly supervised and are not producing very effectively. At the upper levels of program organization, decisions are constantly being taken on the basis of very limited information. Thus there is a real need to increase incentives for good performance and to make major investments in evaluation. Reforms are presently being made in the Program that will gradually bring about some of the changes we are suggesting, but they are not coming fast enough to reduce the birth rate to twenty-five per thousand over the next few years. For that kind of goal to be accomplished it will be necessary to have much more rapid change.

NOTES

1. See Sloan R. Wayland, "Family Planning and the School Curriculum," in *Family Planning and Population Programs*, edited by Bernard Berelson (Chicago: University of Chicago Press, 1966), p. 353. Wayland makes the point that you can work toward influencing family size norms without placing the emphasis on sex education. The literature on population education has recently been reviewed by Ozzie G. Simmons, "Population Education: A Review of the Field," *Studies in Family Planning*, 52, April 1970.
2. There has been considerable discussion of the subject outside India. See Stephen Enke's writings cited in Chapters I and II, or Davis,

"Population Policy: Will Current Programs Succeed?" See also Lenni W. Kangas, "Integrated Incentives for Fertility Control," *Science*, Vol. CLXIX, No. 3952, September 25, 1970, and Edward Pohlman, *Incentives and Compensation in Population Control*, Carolina Population Studies Center, Monograph (forthcoming).

3. Ronald G. Ridker, "Synopis of a Proposal for a Family Planning Bond," *Studies in Family Planning*, 43, June 1969, pp. 11–16.

4. See Institute of Applied Manpower Research, *Manpower Requirements of the Family Planning Programme*, I.A.M.R. Working Paper No. 1/1968, New Delhi, 1968.

5. These remarks are based on data gathered on visits to State Headquarters or contained in the monthly bulletin mimeographed by the Central Government.

6. Government of India, Ministry of Education, *Report of the Education Commission, 1964–1966* (New Delhi, 1967), p. 302.

7. Government of India, Planning Commission, *The Fourth Five Year Plan, A Draft Outline*, p. 339.

8. See the United Nations, Commission for Technical Assistance Department of Economic and Social Affairs, *Report on the Family Planning Programme of India* (New York, February 1966), pp. 50–56.

9. See Chapter VIII for a discussion of this topic.

10. See Simmons, "The Indian Investment in Family Planning," Chapter XV, for a discussion of para-medical insertion of the IUD.

11. In Haryana this referal system—or rather its absence—is a real difficulty. Medical personnel have not always been as cooperative as they might have been in this respect.

12. Doctors are now paid Rs. 30 for any vasectomy they certify having done and Rs. 12 for each IUD insertion.

13. Regular extension workers bring in about four cases per month. They are paid about Rs. 200 per month. Thus the extension effort costs about five times as much per case in Maharashtra as it does in Madras. The canvasser system has been discussed by Robert Repetto, "India: A Case Study of the Madras Vasectomy Program," *Studies in Family Planning*, 31 (May 1968), pp. 8–16. Some of the problems with the Madras canvasser system are reported in K. Srinivasan and M. Kachirayan, "Vasectomy Follow-up Study: Findings and Implications," *Institute of Rural Health and Family Planning Bulletin*, 3, No. 1 (July 1968), pp 20–21. My knowledge of the Madras program has been considerably enhanced by the unpublished work of Jason Finkle.

14. Out of an estimated requirement of 1,675 vehicles, 780 were in use during 1967. Government of India, Ministry of Health and Family Planning, *Report, 1966–1967* (New Delhi, 1967), p. 210.

15. The conflict between these roles and the usual resolution of the conflict through emphasis on the curative aspects of medicine (at the expense of administration) is described in Harbans S. Takulia, Carl E. Taylor, S. Prakash Sangal, and Joseph D. Alter, *The Health Center Doctor in India* (Baltimore: The Johns Hopkins Press, 1967).

16. See the Appendixes in Raina, *Family Planning Programme, Report for 1962–63.*

17. See Joan P. Mencher, "Family Planning in India: the Role of Class Values," *Family Planning Perspectives,* 2, No. 2 (March 1970), pp. 35–39.

18. Myrdal, *Asian Drama,* Prologue.

19. S. N. Agarwala makes the same case in "India's Population Growth and Family Planning Strategy," *Rajasthan Medical Journal,* 5 (March 1965), p. 64; and in *Some Problems of India's Population,* pp. 150–151. The general case against the medical bias in family planning programs is made by J. Mayone Stycos, "A Critique of the Traditional Planned Parenthood Approach in Underdeveloped Areas," in *Research in Family Planning,* edited by C. Kiser (Princeton, N.J.: Princeton University Press, 1962), pp. 477–502.

CHAPTER EIGHT

Population Growth and The Indian Five Year Plans

THE ANALYSIS of the preceding chapters has brought us to the conclusion that population is a crucial factor in India's economic development, that the value of preventing a birth is high, and that returns to investments in family planning are large. We have described how the Indian government, in an effort to counteract the continuing population growth, instituted a family planning program equipped with increasingly large resources. However, the resources were only partially used and the Program, in general, has had but limited success in effecting its goal of reducing the birth rate. Some of the internal problems that inhibited the effectiveness of the Family Planning Program were discussed in Chapter VII. The problems of family planning, however, extend beyond the Program itself, and in order to gain a clear understanding of the recent history of family planning policy, it is necessary to examine the interrelationships between the Program and external institutions. The Planning Commission is given the task of formulating plans "for the most effective and balanced use of the country's resources." Consequently, the following discussion focuses on the key role played by the Planning Commission in developing a policy towards family planning. Our fundamental theme is that until the results of the 1961 Census were known, family planning was a low priority investment. During the past ten years there has been an increased recognition, reflected primarily in increased budget allocations, that family planning investments are a useful complement to conventional economic investments. However, population control still does not play a central role in planning models, and even today there seems to be a considerable amount of private soul searching among influential Indians concerning the role the Program might play.

There is a long delay between the initial formulation of a policy and its eventual implementation. Given the importance of research and training, the gestation period is especially long in family planning. Consequently, the programs in existence today are in many respects a reflection of decisions taken years ago. These lags make it especially important to understand the reasons for the low salience of family planning during the first decade of planning. While certain sections of the Five Year Plans gave a great deal of verbal support to the importance of reducing the birth rate, these statements were not followed by the necessary policies. Moreover, forceful implementation was not provided for policies that had been worked out. Among the press of more immediate demands, family planning was given a low priority. Moreover, both the inadequate demographic data and the formal planning models accepted by the Planning Commission precluded the complete integration of family planning with other development activities.

The Indian leadership had an early commitment to a government program for population control. In this respect India was well in advance of most of the countries of the world. But it is one thing to enunciate a population policy, and it is quite a different thing to make the commitments in terms of economic and political resources that could make the announced policy a success. Virtually every government in the world has policies on the books which it does not seek actively to implement. The Indian leadership is not unique in this respect. What we are seeking to point out is that by neglecting to implement fully its announced population policy, the Indian government especially in the early years was missing an opportunity to make a contribution to the attainment of many other goals.

POPULATION GROWTH AND POLICY IN THE PLANS

A fundamental difficulty in dealing with Indian planning is that there is often an enormous discrepancy between the priorities announced in the plan documents and the pattern of allocations of money and effort which results during the process of implementation. The authors of the Indian plans have demonstrated a keen ability to recognize major problem areas within the Indian economy, but they have not always been able to find solutions for them. As a result, there is a wide gap between the ideal world of development mirrored in the plan documents and the actual implementation which The Plan receives during its five years of life.

Population growth has been recognized in the formal documents as one of the important factors determining the rate of economic development. The First Five Year Plan suggested that, apart from the social and institutional environment, the three most important factors determining the rate of economic development are the marginal rate of investment, the incremental capital-output ratio, and the rate of growth of population.

> If population is growing at a certain rate, the total national output has to be raised at the same rate merely to maintain existing standards of income and consumption; this means that not only

will so much less of further additions to national income be available for ploughing back into investment but a part of what is ploughed back will be taken up by capital equipment required for maintaining per capita incomes constant in the following period. It is true that a growing population increases the manpower potential of the country and also has the effect, in some ways, of stimulating investment. It is also true that the effect of an increase in population cannot be judged solely in terms of the effect on per capita incomes; it affects the whole pattern of production and consumption.[1]

The chapter on public health in the First Five Year Plan suggests that the birth rate will be unlikely to fall of its own accord and, consequently, that family planning should be a part of the public health program. In the later plans, an increasing emphasis was placed on the need for a strong population policy. In the Second Five Year Plan the discussion was moved from the chapter on public health to the introduction.

> While there may be differences as to the likely rates of population growth over the next 20 to 25 years, indications clearly are that even with the utmost effort which can be made—and has to be made—at this stage to bring down the birth-rates, population pressure is likely to become more acute in the coming years. This highlights the need for a large and active programme aimed at restraining population growth, even as it reinforces the case for a massive developmental effort.[2]

The Third Five Year Plan goes so far as to state that "the objective of stabilizing the growth of the population over a reasonable period must therefore be at the very center of planned development."[3] The Fourth Five Year Plan indicates a greatly increased allocation of funds for family planning, and in its prefatory remarks implies the continuation of the commitments made to family planning in The Third Plan.

> If population keeps growing rapidly, the major part of investment and national energy and effort may be used up for merely main-

taining the existing low living standards. Population growth thus presents a very serious challenge. It calls for a nation-wide appreciation of the urgency and gravity of the situation. A strong, purposeful Government policy, supported by effective programme and adequate resources of finance, men and materials is an essential condition of success.[4]

THE CONDUCT OF POLICY

It is clear from the above citations that, on paper at least, Indian planners recognized the importance of population growth and were prepared to adopt an active population policy. However, in spite of the formal attention that population received in the plans, demographic matters in general, and the Family Planning Program in particular, were accorded less attention than one would have expected. We will discuss first the treatment of demographic data and, second, the allocation of funds to the Family Planning Program.

India is a very poor country, and its statistics are inadequate in many ways. Indian planners recognized the lack of demographic data, and they approved in the First Five Year Plan a program for improving vital statistics. Either the program was never implemented or it was unsuccessful, for the registration of vital events in 1970 is nearly as lacking as it was in 1951. There is still no way of determining the current rate of growth of the population for any single state, much less for the country as a whole. In the absence of reasonable vital statistics, planners were obliged to resort to alternative sources of information. It is interesting to examine how they chose the estimates they used.

Table VIII-1 summarizes the data available to planners on the basis of the census. The reverse survival method has been used to compute the vital rates. On the basis of information available from the 1951 Census, the planners assumed that the average annual rate of natural increase between 1951 and 1960 would be 1.25 percent, or 12.5 per thousand, the average annual rate of increase for the previous decade. Since the 1941–1950 rate of population growth was not the highest ever recorded, and since it was known that there were factors which kept mortality higher during that decade than would have been expected during the first decade of planning, it is difficult to appreciate what made the Planning Commission expect population to continue to grow at a rate of 1.25 percent per year. Surely the public health programs of the First Five Year Plan could have been expected to reduce mortality by a significant amount.

The Second Five Year Plan had five more years and more knowledge behind it. There had been no census since 1951, but a number of demographic studies had been published which indicated that the birth rate was higher than previously thought. The Planning Commission expressed some doubt as to whether the rate of growth assumed in the First Five Year Plan were not too low, but decided that "for the

TABLE VIII-1

POPULATION INCREASE AND
VITAL RATES FROM THE CENSUS

Year (1)	Population (millions) (2)	Percent Growth (3)	Computed Birth Rate (per thousand) (4)	Computed Death Rate (per thousand) (5)
1901	236			
1911	252	+ 5.73	49.2	42.6
1921	251	− 0.31	48.1	47.2
1931	279	+11.01	46.4	36.3
1941	319	+14.22	45.2	31.2
1951	361	+13.31	39.9	27.4
1961	439	+21.50	41.7	22.8

Sources:
  Columns (2) and (3): *Census of India: Paper No. 1 of 1962*, 1961 Census, Final Population Totals (Delhi, 1962), pp. 8–9.
  Columns (4) and (5): Government of India, The Registrar General, *Vital Statistics of India for 1961* (New Delhi, 1964), p. XLII.

period 1951–60 the assumption of a 12.5 percent rate of growth over the decade could perhaps be retained."[5] For the decade 1961–70, the Planning Commission suggested that the annual rate of natural increase might reach 13.3 per thousand, and for 1971–80 they favored 14.0 per thousand per year.

The Planning Commission labored under the difficulty of having no adequate source of data at its disposal. The Indian Census is traditionally taken every ten years, and the Planning Commission did not consider it desirable to alter the pattern.[6] They did, however, make some limited independent studies[7] to supplement the registration system, but the results were not striking enough to convince the Planning Commission to change the estimates upon which the Second Plan was based. Later during the plan period, the preliminary results of the Sample Survey study of fertility and Coale and Hoover's analysis of population growth in India became available. The new information led to rethinking among Indian planners and demographers. In 1959 at a seminar on "Population Growth and India's Economic Development,"[8] the experts agreed that India's 1961 population would be larger than the 408 million projected in the Second Five Year Plan. Some of them guessed that the population might be as high as 420 or 425 million at the time of the 1961 census. The actual figure was later revealed to be 438 million. The upward revision of the planner's estimate of the total population and the growth rate which were necessary between the Draft Outline of the Third Plan (1960) and the actual plan (1961) meant that both the level of per capita income for 1961, the base year of the plan, and the projected rate of growth of per capita income during the plan period had to be scaled down. Lewis notes that "the planners plainly were shaken by the unexpectedly high census figures."[9]

The lack of adequate information is an obstacle to progress on all levels. It makes it difficult to assess the relative priority that should be accorded "the population problem" among the many conflicting demands for scarce resources, and it increases the difficulty of making decisions within the Program. Many observers of Indian policy making have suggested that the data problem is characteristic of economic planning in general. Thus, Lipton and Streeten in the introduction to a series of essays on Indian planning proclaim, "A fundamental line of criticism emerges from this book. It avers that Indian planners rely too much on bad data. . ."[10]

As is indicated in Table IV-1, the amount of money allocated to support the population policy described in the plans has been until recently relatively small. In the First Plan less than $2 million was allocated for controlling fertility in all of India, and more important still, less than one quarter of the amount allotted was spent. During the later plans, larger amounts were designated for family planning, but at no time did family planning consume a large proportion of plan outlays. For the Third Plan, it was 16 out of 10,400 crores rupees for the entire Plan; that is, expenditures on family planning represented only 0.16 percent of the total. In the final version of the Fourth Five Year Plan, expenditure on family planning for the five years of the plan is projected to be Rs. 315 crores out of a total of Rs. 24, 882 crores. Thus a vastly expanded expenditure on family planning still represents only 1.3 percent of all plan expenditure.

Lack of financing in the early period is not the only indication of the lack of urgency with which the Planning Commission treated the question of population policy. The Program was relegated to the care of the Health Ministry, away from the mainstream of developmental activities. The government was relatively conservative in determining which contraceptive techniques could be used in the Program. There have been restrictions on the use of publicity. Program administration has been neglected, and the Program has not been until recently subjected to the close scrutiny given many other developmental activities. At different points in the past, leaders with both weak commitment to family planning and little influence in government have been given control of the Program. Many of the more recent difficulties of personnel, administration and evaluation were described in the last chapter. The important point is that, if the program had been given top priority and if the Planning Commission had committed itself to success at any cost, then many of the problems might have been resolved more quickly.[11]

It is important to attempt to establish the reasons for the discrepancy between the priority given demographic problems on paper and the low salience they seem to have had in the actual implementation of policy. There appear to be two fundamental reasons for the discrepancy. First, although per capita income has been indicated to be the major goal of Indian economic planning, it seems likely that the major operational goal is total national income. Second, the early plans were based on demographic and economic models which did not leave any role for population policy. The importance of these two factors is illustrated by the different estimates of the value of preventing a birth which are given in Table II-2. It will be noted that when one takes aggregate national income as the goal of economic policy and when one assumes that there is no functional relationship between population growth and that goal, then there is no value to preventing a birth. Different goals and different assumptions concerning the interaction between population and economic growth indicate that the value of preventing a birth is quite high.

The principal announced goal of economic planning is to improve the standard of living of the Indian masses. Lewis contends that the basic strategy of planning is:

> to promote a stated minimum increase in real income per capita. . . . It is the considered judgment of the Indian government and parliament that no lesser rate of improvement is apt to support the maintenance of orderly political processes.[12]

The consequences in terms of achieving a targeted gain in per capita income of discovering that the decennial rate of increase of population is 72 percent larger than planned are grave. The consequences for employment or the projection of the pattern of demand are no less important. It is difficult to attach a money value to the misestimation of this parameter, but if the per capita income goal is really as important as Lewis suggests, it is certainly great enough to warrant the costs of a more extended data collecting effort. Lewis may have overstated the importance attributed by the Indian planners to per capita income. Per capita income may be indicated in the plan documents as the chief goal of planning, but total production is the announced goal of the relevant models. There is then an intellectual basis for the low priority given to family planning.

In the discussion that follows it is contended that the low value attached to knowing the real rate of population increase and the small amount of money and effort allocated to family planning during the early phase result from the use of planning models where population is of little importance and demographic models where fertility is a function of income.

India has now had over fifteen years of experience with planned economic development. The three plans which have been completed vary with regard to the ambitiousness of the goals which they contain and the strategies which they embody. The First Five Year Plan is usually thought to have been a collection of projects with little recognized interdependence. To the extent that there is a formal model underlying the plan it is of the simple Harrod-Domar sort which would permit the planners to calculate the necessary rate of investment for a given rise in income and vice versa. The First Five Year Plan aimed at only a modest 11 percent increase in national income and concentrated its investment in the agricultural sector. The Second Five Year Plan was much more ambitious. It aimed at increasing national income by 25 percent and allocated a very large part of total expenditures to industrial projects. The author of the model on which the Second Plan is based is Professor Mahalanobis, a *de facto* member of the Planning Commission who is usually thought more than anyone else to be responsible for the shape of Indian planning after the First Plan.

The Mahalanobis model consists of a set of simultaneous equations specifying the relationships between investment, employment, and increased output in a four-sector economy. There is one sector producing investment goods; the other three produce consumer goods. The unknowns in the system are the allocations to the three consumer goods sectors. The rate of investment in the investment goods sector is a political decision. The purpose of the model is to stipulate that pattern of investment allocation which will produce a targeted rate of national income growth and a targeted number of new jobs. The model is simple as policy-making models go, and its lack of complexity is perhaps the source of the major criticisms which have been levied against it.[13] Many of the more interesting aspects of an economy are not made a part of the model. There is no saving function; imports are assumed not to exist; technological progress is not permitted; there is no demand function, no prices, no gestation lag for investments, no effective administrative constraint. It has even been suggested that the Mahalanobis model does not minimize the resource requirements for producing the targeted income growth and new employment.

A plan which bases its investment allocation on a model which has no savings function, and no built-in demand equations and which targets growth rates in terms of total national income is unlikely to pay much heed to demographic factors. In such a model there is no specification of relationships involving population even as a datum. Employment and national income are both considered to be functions of investments which are determined by the choice of the government. From the point of view of the problems discussed here, the Mahalanobis model could be improved by setting the targets specifically in terms of per capita income or the percentage of the labor force employed and specifying a new relationship between the rate of population growth and the pattern of investment allocation.

The reason for placing so much emphasis on Mahalanobis' early efforts at model construction is that his work seems to have established a pattern which has been continued right up to the present. The Planning Commission has set the tone in making decisions concerning investment priorities. In the process, their principle concern has been with the enormously difficult and important task of determining the conventional investments. As Bhagwati and Chakravarty put it in their review of the models used as theoretical under-pinning for the plans,

> . . . The models which have been developed so far, while they range considerably in their sophistication from simple to very elaborate constructs, have, however, been essentially concerned with the implications of the shortage of capital and foreign ex-change rather than with a full analysis of the abundance of one important factor of production, e.g., unskilled human labor.[14]

The Planning Commission understandably placed top priority with the politically sensitive parts of the plan which they thought most important, such as the relative portions of investment in the public and private sectors, the total rate of income growth, and the degree of concentration on heavy industry. Fertility control did not play an important role in the Mahalanobis model, and it was not the kind of investment which would catch the eyes of planners who had learned their scale of preferences by reading about economic growth in the West or in the Soviet Union. Industrialization and the "socialist pattern of society" were considered more important than the growth of per capita income. The words of the plan documents say that many of the goals of Indian planning are in per capita terms, but planners seem to have been much more interested in the totals.

The views of Professor Mahalanobis on the subject of population control are relevant. They are somewhat difficult to research, since the subject is not mentioned in most of his writing on planning. On the basis of personal correspondence with Mahalanobis, Enke[15] has concluded that Mahalanobis does not consider population growth to be a problem in a country which is rapidly industrializing. The rapid increase of national income will lead to the fall of the birth rate while at the same time it makes that fall less important. Mahalanobis has described his understanding of the relationship between the growth of income and that of population in the introduction to the Sample Survey study of couple fertility.

> The effect, if any, of a rising level of living on the growth of population in India has a direct bearing on national planning. . . . if there exists a peak level of number of children born (or surviving) at a critical level of living then special efforts to increase the income of those households which are below the critical level may turn out to be the most effective approach to a basic solution of the population problem in India and also of the problem of poverty at the same time.[16]

These conclusions are based on a study which is defective in many ways; but the fact that Mahalanobis would see fit to use the results to draw the sanguine conclusion of the quotation just illustrates the strength of his conviction.

The declared willingness of a government to consider adopting a fertility control program does not mean that such a program will be adopted or that if adopted it will be pushed energetically. Before this can happen, those persons in positions of authority must have concluded that population is a real problem and that a fertility control program might do something to alleviate the problem. The views of Professor Mahalanobis indicate that at least one of the leaders influential in establishing planning in India did not consider population a high priority and that, to the extent that he saw a problem, he thought industrialization would be sufficient cure. T. J. Samuel has shown that during the early period at least, Mahalanobis' views were shared by a number of influential government leaders including many who were members of the Planning Commission.[17]

In conclusion it can be said that Indian planning during its first decade of existence paid much less attention to population growth than one would expect in view of the problem or after reading the plan documents. This unconcern with population growth was not primarily the result of oversight or neglect on the part of the planning authorities.[18] To the contrary, it seems to have been the considered view of at least some Indian leaders that population was not really an important problem for planners.

The situation has greatly improved in recent years. As indicated in Table IV-1, the allocation for Family Planning in the Fourth Five Year Plan is enormously increased over earlier plans.[19] Under present circumstances there is no shortage of funds for family planning in India. The problem is to find means of utilizing the available funds. Over the next few years the best way to assess the priority given to Family Planning will not be to examine the financial allocations, but rather to see to what extent the commitment of other resources—effective management, strong leadership, etc.—matches the more than adequate finances. Moreover, recent changes have brought new leaders into the Planning Commission who have a long-standing commitment to the importance of population control as a means of securing economic advance. Thus some of the conclusions of this chapter may apply with full force only to the earlier period of Indian planning. The battle is by no means over, but it is hopeful to think it may at last be engaged.

NOTES

1. Government of India, Planning Commission, *First Five Year Plan* (New Delhi, 1952), p. 18.
2. Government of India, Planning Commission, *Second Five Year Plan* (New Delhi, 1956), p. 7.

3. *Third Five Year Plan*, p. 25.
4. Government of India, Planning Commission, *Fourth Five Year Plan* (New Delhi, 1969), p. 32.
5. *Second Five Year Plan*, p. 8. In the text, as indicated, the rate is said to be 12.5 percent per *decade*, but in the *First Five Year Plan* and in the tables, the rate is 1.25 percent per *annum*. As stated in the *Second Five Year Plan* text, the rate would be even lower than that calculated for 1941–50. It is interesting in this regard to notice that there is nothing very sacred about the estimate of a birth rate of 39.9 per thousand. When Coale and Hoover, *Population Growth and Economic Development*, suggested that the birth rate was probably higher than that, S. P. Jain, the 1951 Census Actuary defended the estimate rather elaborately in his contribution to a conference; see Agarwala, *India's Population*. However, after the results of the 1961 Census were out, Jain, himself, calculated an alternative set of birth rates higher than those calculated earlier for 1951. See Government of India, Office of the Registrar General, *Vital Statistics for India of 1961*.
6. The U.N. Advisory group has recommended the possible adoption of a census every five years. U.N., *An Evaluation of the Family Planning Program of the Government of India*, p. 80.
7. The Census Commissioner undertook a series of special studies in 1952–53, the results of which were defective. The results were accurate enough to indicate that the birth rate was certainly not falling, and was probably higher than previously thought, while the death rate was probably lower. See Census Commissioner, *Census of India, Paper No. 1* and *Paper No. 2*, New Delhi, 1955. The studies of the Gokhale Institute were also published before the preparation of the Second Plan, and they also indicated birth rates above 40 per thousand. Moreover, preliminary results from the Seventh and Eighth Rounds of the National Sample Survey which indicated a rate of natural increase of 1.6 percent per year and of the Ninth and Tenth Rounds (1955–56) which indicated a rate of natural increase of 1.8 percent were presumably available at the time the Second Five Year Plan was finalized.
8. Reported in S. N. Agarwala, *India's Population*, (Bombay: Asia Publishing House, 1962).
9. John P. Lewis, *Quiet Crisis in India* (Washington, D.C.: The Brookings Institution, 1962), p. 76.
10. Michael Lipton and Paul Streeten, "Two Types of Planning" in *The Crisis of Indian Planning*, edited by Michael Lipton and Paul Streeten, (London: Oxford University Press, 1968), p. 7. *See also*

Wilfred Malenbaum, *Prospects for Indian Development*, (London: George Allen and Unwin, 1962), pp. 62–64; Myrdal, *Asian Drama*, pp. 481–83, and A. H. Hanson, *The Process of Planning*, (London: Oxford University Press, 1966), p. 63.

11. For a discussion of the political aspects of population control through 1958, see R. A. Gopalaswami, "Administrative Implementation of Family Planning Program," *Population Review* (January, 1959).

12. John P. Lewis, *Quiet Crisis in India*, pp. 23, 25.

13. P. C. Mahalanobis, "Some Observations on the Process of Growth of National Income," *Sankhya*, 12 (1952), pp. 307-312; "The Approach of Operational Research to Planning in India," *Sankhya*, 16 (1955), pp 3–62; "Draft Plan Frame for the Second Five-Year Plan," *Sankhya*, 16 (1955), pp. 63–89. Mahalanobis has discussed some of his ideas on planning in the collected papers, *Talks on Planning* (Asia, 1961). Critical reviews of his ideas are to be found in the following: R. Komiya, "A Note on Professor Mahalanobis' Model of Indian Economic Planning," *Review of Economics and Statistics*, 41 (February 1959), pp. 29–35; M. Bronfenbrenner, "A Simplied Mahalanobis Development Model," *Economic Development and Cultural Change*, 9 (October 1960), pp. 45–51; M. Chand, "Models for Planning in a Socialist Economy with Reference to India's Second Five Year Plan," *Indian Journal of Economics*, 39 (July 1958), pp. 105–122; M. Kant "Some Structural Aspects of Mahalanobis' Four-Sector Model," *Indian Journal of Economics*, 41 (April 1961), pp. 313–322; Malenbaum, *Prospects for Indian Development*, pp. 86 ff.

14. Jagdish N. Bhagwati and Sukhamoy Chakravarty, "Contributions to Indian Economic Analysis: A Survey," *The American Economic Review*, Vol. LIX, No. 4, Part 2, Supplement, Sept. 1961, pp. 2–73.

15. Stephen Enke, "Some Reactions to Bonuses of Family Limitation," *Population Review* (July 1961), p. 35.

16. The National Sample Survey, Number 7, *Couple Fertility*, by A. Das Gupta, *et al.*, published in *Sankhya*, 16 (April 1956). Foreword by Mahalanobis, p. 235.

17. T. J. Samuel, "The Development of India's Policy of Population Control," *The Milbank Memorial Fund Quarterly*, Vol. XLIV, No. 1, Part 1, Jan. 1966, pp. 49–67. See also Myrdal, *Asian Drama*, Chapter 28, and Appendix 12.

18. Little says of the population policy of the Third Five Year Plan that, "the lack of an adequate response to this fairly recent realization that a population explosion is already taking place seems to

proceed not from any religious distaste or lack of intellectual conviction, but from a normal government tendency to do too little too late and hope for the best." I. M. D. Little, "India's Third Five Year Plan," *Oxford Economic Papers*, 14 (February 1962), pp. 1–24.

19. Asoka Mehta and D. R. Gadgil, the two most recent Deputy Chairmen of the Planning Commission, are both on record favoring family planning. Asoka Mehta, *The Plan: Perspective and Problems* (Bombay: Bharatiya Vidya Bhavan, 1966) Chapter 14; D. R. Gadgil, *Planning and Economic Policy in India* (Bombay: Asia Publishing House, 1965), p. 209. One of the Planning Commission members with very long association with planning has recently written an article which may reflect the new attitude of economic planners to family planning. See Pitambar Pant, "Population, Economic Development and Food," *Seminar*, June 1970.

CHAPTER NINE

Conclusions

THE CONTROL of population growth will not in and of itself assure the success of India's developmental effort. Major transformations of the economic, social and political structure will be necessary for that to occur. But some form of population control will have to be a part of the solution. The success or failure of the Indian Family Planning Program will be of major consequence for the history of mankind. If it succeeds in reducing the birth rate to the targeted level of twenty-five per thousand in the near future, India may well be able to make the leap into a condition where all of its citizens enjoy "the good life"—where each citizen of India has enough to eat and where there is a wide range of dignified and culturally acceptable alternatives open to all. If it does not succeed, the misery of India's poor and the unhappy, locked-in quality that characterizes many aspects of life in India is likely to continue much longer than it should.

India was the first country in the world to initiate an official, government-directed effort to limit its birth rate. In making this decision, Indian policy makers were committing themselves to the view that the rate of population growth is *not* determined by forces beyond all control. They were asserting that social intervention in the shape of the

193

Family Planning Program would be able to exert some influence on human fertility. One major purpose of the present study has been to catalogue the successes and failures of this bold venture.

The Program has now reached middle age. Annual expenditures have grown by leaps and bounds. In an absolute sense—measured by the number of births prevented or the rupee value of the resulting benefits—its successes are impressive, but when measured against its potential, they do not seem so outstanding. The acceptors of the IUD and sterilization are still only a small portion of the entire population of eligible couples in India. A beginning has been made, but it is our feeling that before the Program will be able to accomplish its immediate goal of reducing the birth rate to twenty-five per thousand, the Indian family must be brought, either by the activities of the government or for quite independent reasons, to attach less value to having large numbers of children. The problem of reducing fertility is more complicated than facilitating access to clinics or providing information about contraceptive technology.

The Family Planning Program is now reaching a massive audience, but it has become somewhat cumbersome. There is a veritable army of employees presently working for the Program at the Center, in the states, and at the local level. The massive dimensions of the family planning effort and the inherent complexity of the task present an enormous challenge to the usual Indian public health administration. If it is to succeed in accomplishing its goals, the program must develop an adequate control system, and the most important element in such a system would be a stream of information sufficient to make the proper decisions and an evaluation framework that will permit a correct ordering of priorities.

It is our contention that the relationship between economic development and population growth is so close that the two are impossible to separate. Two important conclusions which derive from this point of view are that economic planners should deal explicitly with population growth and control in their models and that family planning should be evaluated in large measure by the contribution it makes to economic development. Thus, our feeling is that it is easiest to judge any portion of the Program—be it choice of technique or the relative success of extension methods—if the criterion for evaluating alternative policies is the contribution they make to India's development effort. For example the relatively high value of a sterilization, as opposed to an IUD insertion, is clearest when one examines the higher economic benefit that it generates for the nation. Similarly, the high cost of administrative deficiencies is more obvious when the Family Planning Program is assessed in economic terms than when one thinks of it as a public health or social reform program. Such is the logic of using the investment framework.

The early chapters of this study used the economic framework to estimate the impact of past efforts in family planning. It is likely that both the data on which the estimates are based and the theoretical relationships which underlie the analysis will be changed as time passes. The method is more important than any particular result, and in future applications of the method it will be important that the data and the analysis be adjusted to reflect the situation under examination as carefully as possible.

Economic evaluation is not an end in itself. It is merely a tool by which progress can be measured and priorities established. Two important results which emerge from our use of this tool should be stressed in this conclusion. First, information has a high economic value. Knowing the differential performance of different geographic regions can help to make corrections in the lagging regions. The early detection of the difficulties of the IUD as it was used in India might have permitted Program administrators to make the kind of corrections that could have saved the day.

Second, the kind of economic analysis which we have explored in earlier chapters is not only a tool for analyzing the consequences of decisions that have already been taken. More important it is a way of helping to make decisions about alternative approaches to the future. But before we can make decisions about alternative ways of trying to solve a problem, we must know something about the likely outcome of each different approach. One cannot use all imaginable ways of convincing people to use family planning simultaneously. Often alternative approaches are mutually exclusive. For example one might argue that we can either rely on a system of private incentives or on a standard bureaucratic structure to bring about changes in behavior. The two forms of organization may be mutually incompatible. And even when alternative approaches are compatible the basic scarcity of resources and the desire to maximize the resulting outputs constrain us to choosing only the most effective. But for economic analysis to help with the choice among the available alternatives we must have something to evaluate. We must know at least in a probabilistic sense what is likely to be the response to these approaches. We can analyze the past history of the program because we know something about what has transpired. The future is more difficult because there are many ways of organizing family planning programs, and one of the least understood phenomena in the whole field is the response that will result from different combinations of the relevant resources. If there is any priority for research in family planning in India, it is the study of the public response to alternative approaches to family planning. This conclusion underlines both the importance of the kind of experiments which have been done under the auspices of the Communications Action Research Program and the need to study the reasons for the success or failure of ongoing programs. Ultimately what we want to know is how and why people behave the way they do—both within the family planning administration and in making family size decisions. When we have this information it will be easy to make decisions that will maximize the contribution of family planning.

Bibliography

1. Agarwala, S. N. "Evaluating the Effectiveness of a Family Planning Programme." In *Research in Family Planning*, edited by C. Kiser, pp. 409–421. Princeton, N.J.: Princeton University Press, 1961.

2. Agarwala, S. N. "A Follow-up Study of Intra-Uterine Contraceptive Device: An Indian Experience." Mimeographed. New Delhi, 1967.

3. Agarwala, S. N. *India's Population*. Bombay: Asia Publishing Co., 1962.

4. Agarwala, S. N. "India's Population Growth and Family Planning Strategy." *Rajasthan Medical Journal*, 5 (March 1965), p. 64.

5. Agarwala, S. N. *Population*. New Delhi: National Book Trust, 1967.

6. Agarwala, S. N. "Population Control in India: Progress and Prospects." *Law and Contemporary Problems*, Summer 1960.

7. Agarwala, S. N. *Some Problems of India's Population*. Bombay: K. K. Vora, 1966.

8. Arriaga, Eduardo E. *Mortality Decline and Its Demographic Effects in Latin America*. Population Monograph Series, No. 6, Institute of International Studies, University of California, Berkeley, 1970.

9. Arriaga, Eduardo, E. and Davis, Kingsley. "The Pattern of Mortality Change in Latin America." *Demography*, 6, No. 3 (August 1969), pp. 223–242.

10. Bean, Lee R. and Seltzer, William. "Couple Years of Protection and Birth Prevented: A Methodological Examination." *Demography* 5, No. 2 (1968), pp. 947–959.

11. Becker, Gary. "An Economic Analysis of Fertility." *Demographic and Economic Change in Developed Countries*, Universities-National Bureau Committee for Economic Research, pp. 209–240. Princeton, N. J.: Princeton University Press, 1960.

12. Becker, Gary. "Investment in Human Capital: A Theoretical Analysis." *Journal of Political Economy,* **70** (October 1962), pp. 9–49.

13. Berelson, Bernard. "Beyond Family Planning." *Studies in Family Planning,* 38 (February 1969), pp. 1–6.

14. Bhagwati, Jagdish N. and Chakravarty, Sukhamoy. "Contribution to Indian Economic Analysis: A Survey." *American Economic Review,* 59, No. 4 (September, 1969), Part 2, Supplement, pp. 2–73.

15. Bhende, Ashash. "A Bibliography of IUCD Studies in India." *Newsletter,* 31, DTRC, Chembur, January 1970.

16. Blake, Judith. "Are Babies Consumer Durables?" *Population Studies,* **22** (March 1968), pp. 5–25.

17. Blake, Judith. "Demographic Science and the Redirection of Population Policy." *Journal of Chronic Diseases,* 18 (1965), pp. 1181–1200.

18. Blaug, Mark. *Economics of Education 1.* Baltimore: Penguin Books, Inc., 1968.

19. Boserup, Ester. *The Conditions of Agricultural Growth.* Chicago: Aldine Publishing Co., 1965.

20. Brahmananda, P. R. Introduction to *Social Aspects of Savings* by V. R. M. Desai. Bombay: Population Prakashan, 1967.

21. Bromfenbrenner, Martin. "A Simplified Mahalanobis Development Model." *Economic Development and Cultural Change,* 9 (October 1960), pp. 45–51.

22. Carlsson, Gösta. "The Decline of Fertility: Innovation or Adjustment Process." *Population Studies,* **20,** No. 2 (November 1966), pp. 149–174.

23. Chand, Mahesh. "Models for Planning in a Socialist Economy with Reference to India's Second Five Year Plan." *Indian Journal of Economics,* 39 (July 1958), pp. 105–122.

24. Chandrasekaran, C. and Freyman, M. W. "Evaluating Community Family Planning Programs." In *Public Health and Population Change: Current Research Issues,* edited by M. C. Sheps and J. C. Ridley, pp. 266–286. Pittsburgh, Pa.: University of Pittsburgh Press, 1965.

25. Chandrasekhar, Sripati. "How India Is Tackling Her Population Problem." *Foreign Affairs,* **47** (October 1968), pp. 138–150.

26. Clark, Colin. *Population Growth and Land Use.* New York: St. Martin's Press, 1967.

27. Coale, Ansley and Hoover, Edgar M. *Population Growth and Economic Development in Low Income Countries.* Princeton, N.J.: Princeton University Press, 1958.

28. Dandekar, Kumudini. *Population Policies*, Background paper, United Nations World Population Conference, 1965.

29. Davis, Kingsley. "The Amazing Decline of Mortality in Underdeveloped Areas." *American Economic Review*, Papers and Proceedings, May 1956, pp. 305–318.

30. Davis, Kingsley. "Population Policy: Will Current Programs Succeed?" *Science*, 158 (November 10, 1967), p. 732.

31. Davis, Kingsley. "Social and Demographic Aspects of Economic Development in India." In *Economic Growth: Brazil, India, Japan*, edited by Simon Kuznets, Wilbert E. Moore, and Joseph Spengler, pp. 263–315. Durham, N.C.: Duke University Press, 1955.

32. Davis, Kingsley. "The Theory of Change and Response in Modern Demographic History." *Population Index*, 29 (October 1963), pp. 345–366.

33. Demeney, Paul. Comment. *Economic Development and Cultural Change*, 8 (July 1961), pp. 641–644.

34. Demeny, Paul. *Demographic Aspects of Saving, Investment Employment and Productivity*. Background paper, United Nations World Population Conference, 1965.

35. Demeny, Paul. "The Economics of Population Control." A paper prepared for the 1969 General Conference of the International Union for the Scientific Study of Population. September 3–11, 1969. London, England.

36. Demeny, Paul. "Investment Allocation and Population Growth." *Demography*, 2 (1965), pp. 203–232.

37. Demerath, Nicholas J. "Family Planning: Plans and Action." *The Indian Journal of Public Administration*, 11 (October–December 1965), pp. 683–697.

38. Denison, E. T. *Why Growth Rates Differ*. Washington, D.C.: The Brookings Institution, 1967.

39. Easterlin, Richard. "Towards a Socioeconomic Theory of Fertility: Survey of Recent Research on Economic Factors in American Fertility." In *Fertility and Family Planning: A World View*, edited by Samuel Behrman, Leslie Corsa, and Ronald Freedman, pp. 127–156. Ann Arbor: University of Michigan Press, 1969.

40. Eckstein, Otto. "A Survey of the Theory of Public Expenditure Criteria." In *Public Finances: Needs, Sources, and Utilization*, edited by J. M. Buchanan. Princeton, N.J.: Princeton University Press, 1961, pp. 439–494.

41. Eizenga, W. *Demographic Factors and Savings*. Amsterdam: North Holland, 1961.

42. Enke, Stephen. "The Economics of Government Payments to Limit Population." *Economic Development and Cultural Change,* 8 (July 1960), pp. 339–348.

43. Enke, Stephen. "The Gains to India from Population Control: Some Money Measures and Incentive Schemes." *Review of Economics and Statistics,* 42 (May 1960), pp. 175–181.

44. Enke, Stephen. Rejoinder. *Economic Development and Cultural Change,* 8 (July 1961), pp. 645–648.

45. Enke, Stephen. "Some Reactions to Bonuses of Family Limitation." *Population Review,* July 1961.

46. Enke, Stephen. "Speculations on Population Growth and Economic Development." *Quarterly Journal of Economics,* 71 (February 1953), pp. 19–35.

47. Enke, Stephen. "Leibenstein on the Benefits and Costs of Birth Control Programmes." *Population Studies,* 24, No. 1 (March 1970), pp. 115–116.

48. Enke, Stephen and Zind, R. G. "Effect of Fewer Births on Average Income." *Journal of Bio-social Science,* I, No. 1 (January 1969), pp. 41–56.

49. Enke, Stephen and Zind, R. G. "Birth Control for Economic Development." *Science* (May 16, 1969).

50. Freedman, Ronald. "The Sociology of Human Fertility: A Trend Report and Bibliography." *Current Sociology,* 10/11 (1961).

51. Freedman, Ronald and Jain, Anrudh, K. "Comparative Fertility of the IUD Acceptors and of All Married Women of Childbearing Age in Taiwan." Taiwan Population Studies, Working Paper No. 3, Population Studies Center, University of Michigan (mimeograph).

52. Freedman, Ronald and Takeshita, John Y. *Family Planning in Taiwan: An Experiment in Social Change.* Princeton, N.J.: Princeton University Press, 1969, pp. 280–291.

53. Freymann, Moye W. "India's Family Planning Program: Some Lessons Learned." In *Population Dynamics,* edited by Minoru Muramatsu and Paul A. Harper, pp. 13–26. Baltimore: The Johns Hopkins Press., 1965.

54. Gadgil, D. R. *Planning and Economic Policy in India.* Bombay: Asia Publishing House, 1965.

55. Galenson, W., and Leibenstein, Harvey. "Investment Criteria, Productivity and Economic Development." *Quarterly Journal of Economics,* 69 (August 1955), pp. 343–70.

56. Gopalaswami, R. A. "Administrative Implementation of Family Planning Program." *Population Review,* January 1959.

57. Gould, Ketayun H. "Family Planning, A Politically Suicidal Issue." *Economic and Political Weekly*, 4, No. 38 (September 20, 1969), pp. 1513–1518.

58. Hagen, Everett E. and Hawryhyshyn, Oli. "Analysis of World Income and Growth." *Economic Development and Cultural Change*, 18, No. 1 (October 1969), Part II, Special Supplement.

59. Hanson, A. H. *The Process of Planning*. London: Oxford University Press, 1966.

60. Heer, David M. and Smith, Dean O. "Mortality Level, Desired Family Size, and Population Increase," *Demography*, 5, No. 1 (1968), pp. 104–121.

61. Hirschleifer, Jack. "Comments." In *Public Finances: Needs, Sources and Utilization*, edited by J. M. Buchanan. Princeton, N.J.: Princeton University Press, 1961.

62. Hirschman, Albert O. *The Strategy of Economic Development*. New Haven: Yale University Press, 1958.

63. India, Census Commissioner, *Census of India Paper No. 1*, New Delhi, 1955.

64. India, Census Commissioner, *Census of India Paper No. 2*, New Delhi, 1955.

65. India, Central Statistical Organization, *Statistical Pocket Book of the Indian Union, 1965*. New Delhi, 1965.

66. "India: The Family Planning Program Since 1965." *Studies in Family Planning*, 35 (November 1968), pp. 1–12.

67. India, Ministry of Education, *Report of the Education Commismission, 1964–1966*. New Delhi, 1967.

68. India, Ministry of Health, Family Planning and Urban Development, Department of Family Planning, "Progress of Family Planning Programme in India." CFPI Reprography Unit. November, 1968.

69. India, Ministry of Health and Family Planning, *Report, 1966–1967*, New Delhi, 1967.

70. India, Ministry of Health and Family Planning, *Report 1965–1966*, New Delhi, 1968.

71. India, Ministry of Home Affairs, Office of the Registrar General, "Revised Population Projections" (June 1964) Mimeographed.

72. India, Planning Commission, *First Five Year Plan*, New Delhi, 1952.

73. India, Planning Commission, *Second Five Year Plan*, New Delhi, 1956.

74. India, Planning Commission, *Third Five Year Plan*, New Delhi, 1961.

75. India, Planning Commission, *Fourth Five Year Plan: A Draft Outline,* New Delhi, 1966.

76. India, Planning Commission, *Fourth Five Year Plan 1969–74: Draft,* New Delhi, 1969.

77. India, Registrar General, *Census of India, 1961 Census, Paper No. 1 of 1962, Final Population Totals,* New Delhi, 1962.

78. India, Registrar General, *Vital Statistics of India, 1961,* Delhi, 1965.

79. Institute of Rural Health and Family Planning, Gandhigram. "A Brief Report on the Study of Persons Who Have Undergone Vasectomy in the Institute Area." Mimeograph.

80. Jain, S. P. "Estimation of Population Growth under Family Planning Programs." *Journal of Family Welfare,* 16, No. 1 (September 1969), pp. 33–47.

81. Jain, S. P. "Programme Planning, Evaluation, and Research." *The Journal of Family Welfare,* 15, No. 3 (March 1969), pp. 15–22.

82. Jones, Gavin. "The Economic Effect of Declining Fertility in Less Developed Countries." An Occasional Paper of the Population Council. New York, 1969.

83. Jones, Gavin and Gingrich, P. "The Effects in Differing Trends in Fertility and of Educational Advance on the Growth, Quality, and Turnover of the Labor Force." *Demography,* 5, No. 1 (1968), pp. 226–248

84. Kangas, Lenni W. "Integrated Incentives for Fertility Control." *Science,* 169, No. 3952, September 25, 1970.

85. Kant, M. "Some Structural Aspects of Mahalanobis', Four-Sector Model." *Indian Journal of Economics,* 41 (April 1961), pp. 313–322.

86. Kapil, K. K. "A Bibliography of Sterilization Studies in India, 1952–1968." *Newsletter,* No. 26, Demographic Training and Research Center, Chembur, October 1968.

87. Kar, S. B. "Evaluating Family Planning Programme." *Swash Hind,* 12, No. 9 (September 1968), pp. 283–286, 301.

88. Kerala, University of, Department of Statistics, Evaluation Study II, "Effectively Sterilized Wives." Mimeographed. Trivandrum, 1966.

89. Komiya, R. "A Note on Professor Mahalanobis' Model of Indian Economic Planning." *Review of Economics and Statistics,* 41 (February 1959), pp. 29–35.

90. Krishnan, R. A. "Report Regarding Follow-up of 1000 Sterilized Fathers." Mimeographed. Madras, 1966.

91. Krueger, Anne O. and Sjastaad, L. A. "Some Limitations of Enke's Economics of Population," *Economic Development and Cultural Change,* **10** (July 1962), pp. 423–426.

92. Kuznets, Simon. "Growth and Structure of National Product, Countries in the ECAFE Region, 1950–51." *Report of the Asian Population Conference and Selected Papers.* United Nations. Economic Commission for Asia and the Far East. New York, 1964.

93. Kuznets, Simon. "Population anl Economic Growth." *Proceedings of the American Philosophic Society,* **3** (June 1967), pp. 170–193.

94. Leasure, J. William. "Factors involved in the Decline of Fertility in Spain." *Demography,* **16**, No. 3 (March 1963), pp. 271–285.

95. Leff, Nathaniel H. "Dependency Rates and Savings Rates." *The American Economic Review,* **59** (December 1969), pp. 886–896.

96. Leibenstein, Harvey. *Economic Backwardness and Economic Growth.* New York: John Wiley and Sons, Inc., 1963.

97. Leibenstein, Harvey. "Why Do We Disagree on Investment Policies for Development?" In *Readings in Economic Development,* edited by Morgan, Bety and Choudhury, pp. 128–143. Belmont, Calif.: Wadsworth, 1963.

98. Leibenstein, Harvey. "More on Pitfalls." *Population Studies,* **24**, No. 1 (March 1970), pp. 117–119.

99. Leibenstein, Harvey. "Pitfalls in Benefit-Cost Analysis of Birth Prevention." *Population Studies,* **23**, No. 2 (July 1969).

100. Lewis, John P. *Quiet Crisis in India.* Washington, D. C.: The Brookings Institution, 1962.

101. Lipton, Michael and Streeten, Paul. "Two Types of Planning." *The Crisis of Indian Planning,* edited by Michael Lipton and Paul Streeten, pp. 3–15. London: Oxford University Press, 1968.

102. Little, S .M. D. "India's Third Five Year Plan." *Oxford Economic Papers,* **14** (February 1962), pp. 1–24.

103. Malenbaum, Wilfred. *Prospects for Indian Development.* London: George Allen and Unwin, 1962.

104. McKean, Roland N. *Public Spending.* New York: McGraw-Hill, 1968.

105. Mahalanobis, P. C. "The Approach of Operational Research to Planning in India." *Sankhya,* **16** (1955), pp. 3–62.

106. Mahalanobis, P. C. "Draft Plan Frame for the Second Five Year Plan." *Sankhya,* **16** (1955), pp. 63–89

107. Mahalanobis, P. C. Forward to "Couple Fertility," National Sample Survey, No. 7, by A. Das Gupta, *et al. Sankhya,* **16** (April 1956).

108. Mahalanobis, P. C. "Some Observations on the Process of Growth of National Income." *Sankhya*, 12 (1952), pp. 307–312.
109. Mahalanobis, P. C. *Talks on Planning.* Asia, 1961.
110. Marglin, Steven A. *Public Investment Criteria: Benefit-Cost Analysis for Planned Economic Growth.* London: George Allen and Unwin Ltd., 1967.
111. Mauldin, W. Parker. "Births Averted by Family Planning Programs." In *Turkish Demography: Proceedings of a Conference,* edited by Frederic C. Shorter and Bozkurt Güvenc. Turkey: Hucettepe University, Institute of Population Studies, 1969, pp. 281–297.
112. Mauldin, W. Parker. "Measurement and Evaluation of National Family Planning Programs." *Demography*, 4, No. 1 (1967), pp. 71–80.
113. Mehta, Asoka. *The Plan: Perspective and Problems.* Bombay: Bharatiya Vidha Bhavan, 1966.
114. Mincer, Jacob. "Market Prices, Opportunity Costs, and Income Effects," in *Measurement in Economics: Studies in Mathematical Economics and Econometrics in Memory of Yehuda Grunfeld.* Stanford: Stanford University Press, 1963.
115. Murphy, K. G. Krishna. *Research in Family Planning in India.* Delhi: Sterling Publishers, 1968.
116. Musgrave, Richard A. "Cost-Benefit Analysis and the Theory of Public Finance," *Journal of Economic Literature,* 7 (September 1969), pp. 797–806.
117. Myrdal, Gunnar. *Asian Drama.* New York: Pantheon, 1968.
118. National Sample Survey, No. 76. *Fertility and Mortality Rates in India.* Delhi, 1963.
119. Notestein, Frank W. "Problems of Policy in Relation to Areas of Heavy Population Pressure." In *Population Theory and Policy,* edited by J. J. Spengler and O. D. Duncan, pp. 470–483. Glencoe, Ill.: Free Press, 1956.
120. Ogale, S. L. "The Role of Extension Education, Incentives and Disincentives in Promoting the Small Family Norm." *The Journal of Family Welfare,* 15, No. 3 (March 1969), pp. 23–30.
121. Ogale, S. L. and Ranganathan, H. N. "Fertility Changes in Some Areas of Maharashtra." *The Journal of Family Welfare* 15, No. 4, (June 1969), pp. 9–17.
122. Ohlin, Goran. *Population Control and Economic Development.* Paris: OECD, 1967.
123. Opler, Morris Edward. "Cultural Context and Population Control Programs in Village India." In *Fact and Theory in Social Science,*

edited by E. W. Count and G. R. Bowles, pp. 201–221. Syracuse, N.Y.: Syracuse University Press, 1964.

124. Pant, Pitambar. "Population, Economic Development and Food." *Seminar*, June 1970.

125. Petersen, William. "The Demographic Transition in the Netherlands." *American Sociological Review*, 25, No. 3 (June 1966), pp. 334–347.

126. Poffenberger, Thomas. "Age of Wives and Number of Living Children of a Sample of Men Who Had the Vasectomy in Meerut District, U.P." *Journal of Family Welfare*, 13, No. 4 (June 1967), pp. 48–51.

127. Poffenberger, Thomas. *Husband-Wife Communication and Motivational Aspects of Population Control in an Indian Village.* Central Family Planning Institute. New Delhi, December 1969.

128. Pohlman, Edward. *Incentives and Compensation in Population Control.* Carolina Population Studies Center, Monograph (forthcoming).

129. Potter, Robert G. "Application of Life Table Techniques to Measurement of Contraceptive Effectiveness." *Demography*, 3, No. 2 (1966), pp. 297–304.

130. Potter, Robert G. "Estimating Births Averted in a Family Planning Program." In *Fertility and Family Planning: A World View*, edited by S. J. Behrman, Leslie Corsa, and Ronald Freedman. Ann Arbor: The University of Michigan Press, 1969. pp. 413–434.

131. Potter, Robert G. "A Technical Appendix on Procedures Used in Manuscript, 'Estimating Births Averted in a Family Planning Program.'" Prepared for Major Ceremony V, University of Michigan Sesquicentennial Celebration. Mimeographel, June 1, 1967.

132. Potter, Robert G., *et al.* "A Case Study of Birth Interval Dynamics." *Population Studies*, 19 (July 1965), pp. 81–96.

133. Prest, A. R. and Turvey, R. "Cost-Benefit Analysis: A Survey." *Economic Journal*, 75 (December 1965), pp. 683–735.

134. Raina, B. L. *Family Planning Programme Report for 1962–63.* Government of India, Directorate General of Health Services, Ministry of Health. New Delhi, 1964.

135. Raina, Bishen L. "India." In *Family Planning and Population Programs*, edited by Bernard Berelson, pp. 111–121. Chicago: The University of Chicago Press, 1966.

136. Rao, Khrishna. "A Study of IUD Cases in Bangalore." *Family Planning News*, 3 (March and April 1968).

137. Raulet, Harry M. "Family Planning and Population Control in Developing Countries." *Demography*, 7, No. 2, pp. 211–234.

138. Repetto, Robert. "India: A Case Study of the Madras Vasectomy Program." *Studies in Family Planning*, 31 (May 1968), pp. 8–16.

139. Robinson, Warren and Horlacker, David. "Evaluating the Economic Benefits of Fertility Reduction." *Studies in Family Planning*, 39 (March 1969), pp. 4–8.

140. Robinson, Warren, *et al.* "A Cost-Effectiveness Analysis of Selected National Family Planning Programs: A Report on Phase II of the Penn State-USAID Population Project 'Cost-Benefit and Cost-Effectiveness Evaluation of Family Planning Programs.'" Pennsylvania State University, Department of Economics. December 1969.

141. Ryder, N. B. "Fertility." In *The Study of Population: An Inventory and Appraisal*, edited by P. M. Hauser and O. D. Duncan. Chicago: The University of Chicago Press, 1959, pp. 426.

142. Samuel, Thomas J. "The Development of India's Policy of Population Control." *The Milbank Memorial Fund Quarterly*, 44, No. 1 (Jan. 1966), pp. 49–67.

143. Samuel, T. J. "Population Growth and Per Capita Income in Underdeveloped Economies." *Asian Economic Review*, 6 (November 1963).

144. Samuel, T. J. "Why Family Planning Has Had No Impact." *Economic Weekly*, (October 17, 1964), p. 1685.

145. Schultz, T. W. "Reflections on Investment in Man." *Journal of Political Economy*, 70 (October 1962), pp. 1–8.

146. Seltzer, William. "Measurement of Accomplishment: The Evaluation of Family Planning Efforts." *Studies in Family Planning*, 53 (May 1970), pp. 9–15.

147. Sen, Dr. (Smt.) Mukta and Sen, Dr. D. K. "Family Planning Practice of Couples of Reproductive Age Group in a Selected Locality in Calcutta—June, 1965." *Journal of Family Planning*, 14, No. 1 (September 1967), pp. 13–24.

148. Simmons, George B. "The Indian Investment in Family Planning." Ph.D. Dissertation, University of California, Berkeley, 1967, Part II.

149. Simon, Julian L. "The Effect of Income on Fertility." *Population Studies*, 23, No. 3 (November 1969), pp. 327–341.

150. Simon, Julian L. "The Value of Avoided Births to Underdeveloped Countries," *Population Studies*, 23, No. 1 (March 1969), pp. 61–68.

151. Solow, Robert M. "Technical Change and the Aggregate Produc-

tion Function." *Review of Economics and Statistics,* 39 (August 1957), pp. 312-320.

152. Spengler, Joseph. "Economics and Demography." In *The Study of Population,* edited by Philip Hauser and O. D. Duncan, pp. 791-831. Chicago: University of Chicago Press, 1959.

153. Spengler, Joseph. "The Economist and the Population Question." *American Economic Review,* 56 (March 1966), pp. 1-24.

154. Spengler, Joseph J. "Population Problem: In Search of a Solution." *Science,* 166, No. 3910 (December 5, 1969), pp. 1234-1238.

155. Spengler, Joseph J. "Values and Fertility Analysis." *Demography* 3, No. 1 (1966), pp. 109-130.

156. Srinivasan, K. and Kachirayan, M. "Vasectomy Follow-up Study: Findings and Implications." *Institute of Rural Health and Family Planning Bulletin,* 3, No. 1 (July 1968), pp. 20-21.

157. Srinavasan, K., Muthiah, A., and Krishnamoorthy, S. "Analyses of the Declining Fertility in Athoor Block." *Institute of Rural Health and Family Planning Bulletin—Gandhigram IV,* No. 3 (June 1969), pp. 28-58.

158. Stolnitz, George J. "The Demographic Transition: From High to Low Birth Rates and Death Rates." In *Population: The Vital Revolution,* edited by Ronald Freedman. New York, Doubleday & Co., Inc., Anchor Books, 1964.

159. Stolnitz, George J. "Estimating the Birth Effects of India's Family Planning Targets: A Report on Statistical Methodology and Illustrative Projections, 1968-78." Mimeograph. Bloomington, Indiana, July-August 1968.

160. Stycos, J. Mayone. "A Critique of the Traditional Planned Parenthood Approach in Underdeveloped Areas." In *Research in Family Planning,* edited by C. Kiser, pp. 477-502. Princeton, N.J.: Princeton University Press, 1962.

161. Sur, K. B. and Mohanty, S. P. "A Bibliography of Cost-Benefit Studies on Family Planning in India." Demographic Training and Research Centre, *Newsletter,* No. 31 (January 1970), pp. 3-10.

162. Taeuber, Irene B. "Demographic Modernization: Continuities and Transitions." *Demography,* 3, No. 1 (1966), pp. 90-108.

163. Thorner, Daniel. "Long-Term Trends in Output in India." In *Economic Growth: Brazil, India, Japan,* edited by S. Kuznets, W. E. Moore, and J. Spengler, pp. 103-128. Durham, N.C.: Duke University Press, 1955.

164. Tietze, Christopher. "Intra-uterine Contraception: Recommended Procedures for Data Analysis." *Studies in Family Planning,* 18 (Supplement), (April 1967), pp. 1-6.

165. Takeshita, John V. and Freedman, Ronald. "Measuring Acceptances in a Family Planning Program: The Decomposition of Rates by Eligibility Criteria." *Demography*, 4, No. 1 (1967), pp. 158–171.
166. United Nations, Department of Social Affairs, Population Division, "The Determinants and Consequences of Population Trends," *Population Studies*, 17, 1953.
167. United Nations, Department of Social Affairs, Population Studies, No. 22, *Age and Sex Patterns of Mortality: Model Life Tables for Under-Developed Countries*, New York, 1955.
168. United Nations, Commissioner for Technical Co-operation, Department of Economic and Social Affairs, *An Evaluation of the Family Planning Programme of the Government of India*, New York, November, 1969.
169. United Nations, Commissioner for Technical Assistance, Department of Economic and Social Affairs, *Report on the Family Planning Programme in India*, New York, February, 1966. Abstracted in *Studies in Family Planning*. No. 56, August 1970, pp. 4–18.
170. Visaria, P. M. "Mortality and Fertility in India, 1951–1961." *Milbank Memorial Fund Quarterly*, 47 (January 1969), pp. 91–116.
171. Wayland, Sloan R. "Family Planning and the School Curriculum." In *Family Planning and Population Programs*, edited by Bernard Berelson. Chicago: University of Chicago Press, 1966.
172. Wishik, Samuel M. "Indexes for Measurement of Amount of Contraceptive Practice." Presented at meeting of Expert Group on Assessment of Acceptance and Use-Effectiveness of Family Planning Methods, United Nations Economic Commission for Asia and the Far East, Bangkok, Thailand, June 11–21, 1968.
173. Zaiden, George C. "Population Growth and Economic Development." *Studies in Family Planning*, 42 (May 1969), pp. 1–6.

Index

211